LA CUCINA ITALIANA

VEGETARIAN

DISHES

LA CUCINA ITALIANA

VEGETARIAN

DISHES

Edited by Judith Ferguson

PRION

Published in the United Kingdom by
PRION,
an imprint of Multimedia Books Limited,
32-34 Gordon House Road, London NW5 1LP

Editors Judith Ferguson, Linda Osband
Design Terry Allen, Megra Mitchell
Jacket design Megra Mitchell
Production Hugh Allan

Original recipes and pictures copyright © NEPI
***La Cucina Italiana*, Via Mascheroni,**
1-20123 Milan
English translation and compilation copyright
© Multimedia Books Limited, 1987, 1992

British Library Cataloguing-in-Publication Data
Vegetarian dishes. – (La Cucina Italiana)
I. Ferguson, Judith II. Series
6541.5945

ISBN 1-85375-039-5

Printed in Italy by New Interlitho

CONTENTS

ANTIPASTI

Italian *antipasti*, meaning literally "before the pasta",
are meant to whet the appetite and are an important way to begin
a meal in Italy. Vegetables are favourite *antipasti* ingredients and,
in more elaborate forms, can be a satisfying meal in
themselves. Italian soups, like the famous *minestrone* with
vegetables and dried beans or pasta, are also quite
substantial and can be sufficient for a main course as well
as a starter.

& SOUPS

Cauliflower à la Grecque

Cavolfiore del Pireo

To serve 4-6

olive oil

juice of 2 large lemons

2 bay leaves

2 garlic cloves

3-4 black peppercorns

1½ lb/750 g cauliflower

Preparation and cooking time: about 1 hour plus chilling

Bring to the boil a large saucepan containing 1½ pints/800 ml cold water, add 6 tablespoons/100 ml of olive oil, the strained lemon juice, 2 bay leaves, 2 large halved garlic cloves, 3-4 black peppercorns and salt.

Meanwhile, wash the cauliflower and separate it into flowerets, without breaking them. Cook in the boiling liquid, with the pan covered and over a low heat, for about 12 minutes.

Remove the pan from the heat and, keeping it covered, let the flowerets cool. Only at this point remove the garlic and peppercorns (leave the bay leaves), then pour the preparation into a salad bowl. Cover it with cling film and keep it in the refrigerator for at least 1½ hours before serving. This starter, keeps well in the refrigerator for up to a week.

Gourmet Asparagus

Asparagi di Bassano alla Buongustaia

To serve 4

2½ lb/1.2 kg fresh asparagus

a few parsley leaves

4 oz/100 g butter

4 egg yolks

Preparation and cooking time: about 45 minutes

Wash and trim the asparagus and tie in a bundle with kitchen twine. Stand the bundle upright in a saucepan of salted boiling water (the water should come about halfway up the asparagus). Simmer over a moderate heat for about 15 minutes, or a little longer if the asparagus are very thick.

Drain thoroughly, discard the kitchen twine and spread the asparagus out to dry on kitchen paper. Arrange in warmed asparagus dishes and garnish with a few leaves of parsley.

Melt the butter, season with salt and pepper and pour into a well in the asparagus in each dish. Place 1 egg yolk in the centre of each well containing the melted butter. Serve immediately. Each diner should blend the butter and egg yolk to form a delicate sauce and use it as a dip.

Cauliflower à la grecque

Savoury Canapés

Tartine Dolcipiccanti

To serve 4

2 oz/50 g butter, cut into small pieces

4 oz/100 g soft Gorgonzola cheese

1 teaspoon lemon juice

1 tablespoon chopped parsley

4 slices white bread

1 red pimiento

1 tender lettuce leaf, cut into strips

Preparation time: about 30 minutes

Beat the butter with a pinch of salt and pepper until creamy. Add the sieved and mashed Gorgonzola cheese and a teaspoon of lemon juice. Stir vigorously for a few minutes and then blend in the chopped parsley. Check and adjust the seasoning according to taste.

Spread the mixture on the slices of bread. Cut each slice in half diagonally to form 2 triangles and arrange on a plate. Cut the pimiento into 8 small strips and use to decorate the canapés. Garnish the centre of the plate with the strips of lettuce and serve immediately.

Lettuce "Cigars"

"Sigari" di Lattuga

To make 24 "cigars"

1 fresh lettuce

5 oz/150 g fresh Ricotta cheese

2 oz/50 g Gorgonzola cheese

1 tablespoon juniper-flavored *grappa* or brandy

dried tarragon

Preparation time: about 25 minutes

Pull out the tender leaves of the heart of the lettuce and wash and dry them gently. Using a sharp knife, remove the central stalks and divide each leaf in half.

Drain and mash the Ricotta and place it in a bowl. Finely dice the Gorgonzola cheese and beat it with the Ricotta to form a smooth, creamy mixture. Stir in the juniper-flavored *grappa,* a pinch of salt and pepper and a generous pinch of dried ground tarragon.

Blend thoroughly and then place a teaspoon of the mixture on each piece of lettuce. Fold up to form cigar-shaped rolls, making sure that the filling does not ooze out.

Arrange the "cigars" around the edge of a plate and garnish the centre as desired. This dish makes an excellent light hors d'oeuvre or can be served with aperitifs.

Lettuce cigars (above); **savoury canapés** *(left)*

Quick Minestrone

Minestrone Rapido con i Ditaloni

To serve 4-6

1 small onion

1 garlic clove

olive oil

½ celery heart

3 small carrots

1 medium courgette

1 small turnip

2 small potatoes

4 oz/100 g peas

6 oz/175 g tinned red kidney beans

4 oz/100 g peeled, puréed tomatoes

2½ pints/1½ litres stock (or use stock cube)

4 oz/100 g fluted ditaloni pasta

1 oz/25 g grated Parmesan cheese

Preparation and cooking time: 1¼ hours

Finely chop the onion with the garlic and fry in 4 tablespoons of olive oil in a large saucepan, taking care not to let the vegetables brown. Meanwhile, clean and dice the celery, carrots, courgette, turnip and potatoes into ¾-inch/2 cm cubes. Add to the onion and leave for a few moments. Add the peas, the beans with their liquid and the tomatoes. Stir with a wooden spoon and simmer for about 10 minutes.

Boil the stock and pour in. Stir, and simmer for about 45 minutes over a moderate heat with the pan covered. Stir 2 or 3 times during cooking. Then add the pasta and stir. Simmer until the pasta is cooked *al dente* and remove from the heat. Add a little freshly ground pepper, 3 tablespoons of olive oil and the grated Parmesan cheese. Serve at once.

Quick minestrone (above);
minestrone with pesto (below)

Minestrone with Pesto
Minestrone al Pesto

To serve 4

1 small onion

2 garlic cloves

butter

1 lb/500 g frozen mixed vegetables

3 stock cubes

1 large potato

15 fresh basil leaves

1 tablespoon pine-nuts

1 oz/25 g grated Parmesan cheese

olive oil

a little chopped parsley

Preparation and cooking time: about 1 hour

Finely chop the onion with a garlic clove, then soften in a pan in a large knob of melted butter and 2 tablespoons of oil; make sure they don't brown. Add the frozen vegetables and fry for a few moments, stirring with a wooden spoon. Pour in 3 pints/1.5 litres of boiling water and crumble in the stock cubes. Peel the potato, chop into 2-3 pieces and add to the *minestrone*; cook covered over a medium heat for about 45 minutes, stirring two or three times.

Meanwhile, place the basil leaves, wiped with a damp cloth, half a large garlic clove, a tablespoon of pine-nuts, a tablespoon of grated Parmesan cheese and a pinch of salt in a mortar. Pound with a wooden pestle, adding, in a trickle, 5 tablespoons of olive oil, until you have obtained a smooth *pesto*.

Remove the pieces of potato from the soup with a slotted spoon, mash them and return them to the soup. Add the *pesto*, stir, pour the *minestrone* into 4 soup bowls and sprinkle with chopped parsley. Serve with more Parmesan cheese.

Farmhouse Soup with Egg
Zuppa Contadina all'Uovo

To serve 4

2 stock cubes

4 oz/100 g butter

4 slices white bread

4 very fresh eggs

2 oz/50 g grated Parmesan cheese

Preparation and cooking time: about 20 minutes

Heat about 2 pints/1 litre of water in a saucepan, dissolve the stock cubes and bring to the boil. Melt half the butter in a large frying pan and fry the 4 slices of bread, lightly browning them on both sides. Place them on a baking tray or plate and keep them hot.

As soon as the stock begins to boil reheat the frying pan in which the bread was fried and melt the remaining butter. When it is bubbling hot, break in the eggs, which have been kept at room temperature until this point, very carefully, so as not to break the yolks, and fry. Do not let the whites become brown and dry. Cook until the yolks are done on the outside but still almost raw inside.

Place a slice of fried bread in each soup plate and sprinkle with a teaspoon of grated Parmesan cheese. Remove the eggs from the frying pan, draining off as much fat as possible. Place an egg on each square of fried bread and then, using a ladle, pour in the soup very carefully at the side of the plate so as not to break the egg.

Farmhouse soup with egg

Pasta and Kidney Bean Soup

Pasta e Fagioli

To serve 6

4 oz/100 g kidney beans

a bunch of fresh parsley

2 large garlic cloves

1 medium onion

1 piece celery heart

4 sage leaves

1 small bay leaf

2 large peeled potatoes

1 medium tomato, skinned

2 stock cubes

4 oz/100 g maltagliati pasta

olive oil

grated Parmesan cheese

Preparation and cooking time: 2½ hours plus overnight soaking

Soak the beans overnight in cold water. The following day, finely chop a handful of parsley together with the garlic, onion and celery. Make a muslin bag for the sage and bay leaf. Place all these ingredients in a saucepan. Drain the beans and add to the rest of the ingredients. Add the potatoes and purée the tomato before adding it.

Pour in 4 pints/2 litres of cold water and crumble in the stock cubes. Bring to the boil, turn the heat down to the minimum, cover and simmer for about 2 hours, stirring from time to time. Then remove the potatoes, purée them with a third of the beans and return them to the saucepan. Stir, bring to the boil and then add the pasta and cook in the uncovered pan, stirring from time to time. Remove the dish from the heat, and add 3 tablespoons of olive oil, 3 tablespoons of Parmesan cheese and a little freshly ground pepper. Sprinkle each portion with chopped parsley and serve immediately.

Rice, Potato and Mushroom Soup

Minestra di Riso, Patate e Funghi

To serve 4-6

1oz/25 g dried cep mushroom caps

3 pints/1.5 litres light stock

1 medium onion

1 garlic clove

1 stick celery

2 oz/50 g butter

olive oil

14 oz/400 g potatoes

4 oz/100 g rice

1 oz/25 g grated Parmesan cheese

ground nutmeg

a little chopped parsley

Preparation and cooking time: about 2 hours including soaking

Soak the dried mushrooms in warm water for about 1 hour. Drain them well and slice thinly. Heat the stock. Finely chop the onion with a garlic clove and the celery. Place the chopped mixture in a saucepan, add 1 oz/25 g of the butter and 2 tablespoons of olive oil, then sauté without browning, stirring.

Peel the potatoes, wash, and cut them into cubes of about ¾ inch/2 cm, add them to the lightly fried mixture together with the mushroom slices and leave for a few moments, then pour in the hot stock. Stir and slowly bring to the boil, then reduce the heat, cover the pan and simmer for 15 minutes.

Mash a few of the potato cubes, pressing them with a wooden spoon against the side of the pan, then add the rice to the boiling soup, stirring with a wooden spoon. Cook over a rather high heat until the rice is *al dente*. Remove the pan from the heat and stir in the rest of the butter, cut in small pieces with the Parmesan cheese and the ground nutmeg. If you like, sprinkle the soup with chopped parsley.

Pasta and kidney bean soup

March Soup

Zuppa Marzolina

To serve 6

1 medium leek

½ celery heart

3 large carrots

1 lb/500 g cauliflower

a piece of dried cep mushroom

1 artichoke

2 oz/50 g butter

olive oil

2 oz/50 g flour

12 oz/350 g small peas

2 stock cubes

6 slices French bread

1 oz/25g grated Parmesan cheese

Preparation and cooking time: about 1¾ hours

Finely slice the leek, dice the celery and carrot and coarsely chop the cauliflower. Crumble the dried mushroom and clean the artichoke, including the stalk. Cut it in half and then into small pieces. Melt 1 oz/25 g of butter in a saucepan with 3 tablespoons of olive oil and gently fry the vegetables, stirring with a wooden spoon. Sift in the flour, stir again and pour in 4 pints/2 litres of boiling water. Stir again, cover the pan and simmer over minimum heat for about 50 minutes. Then add the peas, and crumble in the stock cubes. Mix and simmer for another 20 minutes or so, keeping the pan covered.

Meanwhile, heat a large pan with the rest of the butter and a tablespoon of oil. Fry the bread until it is golden brown, then place in the bottom of a soup tureen and sprinkle with the Parmesan cheese. Remove the soup from the heat, taste and add salt if required. Stir in a little freshly ground pepper and a thin trickle of olive oil. Then pour the soup over the bread. Wait for a few minutes before serving.

Cream of Carrot Soup

Crema di Carote

To serve 4

8 oz/200 g small tender carrots

2 oz/50 g butter

1 oz/25 g flour

1½ pints/750 ml milk

1 stock cube

2 egg yolks

¼ pint/150 ml fresh whipping cream

ground nutmeg

croûtons

Preparation and cooking time: about 1 hour

Scrape and wash the carrots, then cut into ¼-inch/1 cm cubes. Plunge them into lightly salted boiling water and boil for 5 minutes, then drain and sauté them in half the butter for a few moments without browning them.

Meanwhile, slowly bring 1½ pints/ 750 ml of milk to the boil. Melt the remaining butter in a small saucepan, add the flour, stirring with a small whisk to prevent lumps forming, then slowly dilute the mixture with the boiling milk, stirring constantly; salt very lightly and add the crushed stock cube. Bring the liquid to the boil, then add the carrot cubes in the butter. Stir and simmer gently for 20 minutes, keeping the pan partly covered.

In a bowl beat the 2 egg yolks with the cream. Remove the soup from the heat, fold in the mixture of egg yolks and cream, taste and add a little ground nutmeg and more salt, if necessary. Accompany this delicate cream soup with bread *croûtons* fried in butter.

March soup

Bean Soup with Sweetcorn

Passato di Fagioli con Maïs

To serve 6

2 sprigs fresh sage, chopped

1 minced garlic clove

1 small onion, sliced

2 small carrots, sliced

1 small stalk celery, sliced

2 oz/50 g butter

olive oil

14oz/400 g cooked or tinned haricot beans

14oz/400 g potatoes, peeled and cubed

1 stock cube

a little ground cinnamon

1 medium tomato, skinned and chopped

1 small onion, chopped

12 oz/350 g tinned sweetcorn, drained

1 oz/25 g grated Parmesan cheese

a little chopped fresh parsley

Preparation and cooking time: about 1½ hours

Sauté the sage, garlic, onion, carrots and celery in 1 oz/25 g of butter and 2 tablespoons of olive oil until the onion is transparent. Add the beans, together with their juice, and the cubed potatoes. Stir and simmer for a few minutes and then add 2½ pints/1.5 litres of boiling water. Season with the crumbled stock cube, a pinch of salt and pepper and a little ground cinnamon. Add the tomato, stir and bring back to the boil. Lower the heat, half-cover the pan and simmer gently for about 45 minutes.

Sauté the onion in the remaining butter and a tablespoon of oil. Add the corn and cook for about 10 minutes, pouring on a little boiling water.

Process the bean soup in a

liquidizer, return it to the pan and bring it back to the boil. Add the onion and corn mixture and cook for a further few minutes. Taste and adjust seasoning.

Remove the pan from the heat and blend in the grated Parmesan cheese and 3 tablespoons of olive oil. Sprinkle with the chopped parsley and serve.

time, and collect it in the pan. Adjust the salt to taste, season with a grinding of pepper and nutmeg. Serve the soup with grated Parmesan cheese and, if you wish, with bread *croûtons* fried in butter.

Cream of Vegetable Soup

Crema di Verdure alla Fantesca

To serve 8

2 medium courgettes

6 oz/175 g Brussels sprouts

1 medium onion

4 oz/100 g tender savoy cabbage leaves

1 large carrot

½ celery heart

butter

olive oil

3-4 pieces dried mushroom

4 pints/2 litres light stock (or use stock cube)

½ tablespoon tomato purée

2 oz/50 g rice

nutmeg

grated Parmesan cheese

croûtons

Preparation and cooking time: about 1½ hours

Wash and drain all the vegetables well, then slice them finely and soften them in a large knob of butter and 3 tablespoons of olive oil in a large pan. Add the pieces of dried mushroom and pour in the stock (which you have first brought to the boil). Stir, and add half a tablespoon of tomato purée, then bring to the boil again. Add the rice, stir with a wooden spoon and simmer gently, with the pan half-covered, for about 1 hour, stirring occasionally.
Liquidize the mixture, a little at a

PASTA

Pasta and pizza are, to most non-Italians, typical Italian dishes.
Although pasta has many names and comes in a variety of
shapes, one kind can easily be substituted for another if you
can't find the exact one given in these recipes. Either fresh or
dried pasta can be used — the result will be just as good.

& PIZZA

Pasta with Courgettes
Pasta con Zucchini

To serve 4

1 lb/500 g courgettes

1 medium onion

a little parsley

1 large garlic clove

olive oil

½ stock cube

12 oz/350 g fresh pasta

a little grated Parmesan cheese

Preparation and cooking time: 45 minutes

Clean the courgettes and trim them. Wash and dry well, cut them into rounds about ¼ inch/5 mm thick. Finely chop the onion, parsley and garlic and fry in 5 tablespoons of olive oil without browning. Then add the courgettes and crumble in the stock cube. Add a little freshly ground pepper. Cover with boiling water and stir well.

Cover the pan and cook over a moderate heat for about 10 minutes until the courgettes are tender and the liquid has been absorbed. Season to taste. Cook the pasta in salted boiling water until it is *al dente*. Drain and stir in 2 tablespoons of olive oil. Mix in the sauce and serve at once with the Parmesan cheese.

Pasta with Turnip Tops
Fettuccia Riccia con Cime di Rapa

To serve 4

2 lb/1 kg turnip tops

4 oz/100 g onion

2 large garlic cloves

olive oil

14 oz/400 g peeled tomatoes

4-5 sprigs fresh coriander

caster sugar

12 oz/350 g scalloped wide pasta noodles (fettuccia)

grated Pecorino cheese

Preparation and cooking time: about 1 hour

Boil a large saucepanful of salted water. Clean and wash the turnip tops and put them in the boiling water for 5-6 minutes. Meanwhile finely chop the onion and 1 garlic clove together and fry in 5 tablespoons of olive oil in a small saucepan. Purée the tomatoes and add to the onion. Season with salt and pepper and add the fresh coriander and a pinch of sugar. Stir and gradually bring to the boil. Turn the heat down low and simmer for about 20 minutes, stirring from time to time.

Remove the turnip tops from the water with a slotted spoon and drain well. Sauté them in a large frying pan in 3 tablespoons of olive oil with 1 lightly crushed garlic clove. Top up the water in the saucepan in which the turnip tops were boiled to make at least 5 pints/3 litres and bring to the boil. Pour in the pasta and cook until it is *al dente*. Drain and put the pasta in the pan with the turnip tops; add the tomato sauce. Sauté for a few minutes then serve with grated Pecorino cheese.

Pasta with courgettes

Pasta Twists with Asparagus Sauce

Fusilli con Asparagi

To serve 1

butter

5-6 green asparagus tips, boiled and cooled

flour

6 tablespoons/100 ml milk

¼ stock cube

grated nutmeg

4 oz/100 g pasta twists (fusilli)

2 tablespoons whipping cream

Preparation and cooking time: about 30 minutes

Melt 1 oz/25 g butter in a small saucepan, add the asparagus tips and sauté gently, making sure that they do not brown. Sprinkle with a little sifted flour, stir and, after a few moments, pour in the hot milk in a trickle. Crumble a quarter of a stock cube and add a pinch of nutmeg. Stirring constantly, bring the sauce to the boil, then remove it from the heat and purée it.

Cook the pasta until *al dente* in plenty of salted boiling water, place the cream of asparagus on a very low heat in the saucepan and reheat gently. Stirring constantly, mix in the cream. Adjust the seasoning to taste. Drain the pasta, but not too thoroughly, pour over it the creamy asparagus sauce and garnish, if you like, with more asparagus tips tossed in a little butter. Serve at once.

Pasta Twists with Tomato Sauce and Peas

Fusilli 'Melchiorre'

To serve 4-5

4 oz/100 g leeks, white part only

1 stalk celery

1 small carrot

olive oil

1 garlic clove

1¼ lb/600 g ripe tomatoes

3-4 basil leaves

granulated sugar

4 oz/100 g fresh peas

1 shallot

butter

¼ pint/150 ml stock (or use stock cube)

14 oz/400 g pasta twists

a little parsley

Parmesan cheese or mild Pecorino cheese, grated

Preparation and cooking time: about 1¼ hours

Finely slice the leek, the celery and the carrot. Soften the vegetables in 4 tablespoons of oil in a pan with a clove of garlic. Remove the garlic once it is browned. Chop the tomatoes in small pieces and add them to the lightly fried vegetables. Stir, flavour with 3-4 leaves of basil, salt, pepper and a pinch of sugar. Stir once more, cover the pan and let the sauce cook for about 25 minutes on a medium heat, stirring occasionally.

Cook the peas in salted boiling water until tender. Meanwhile finely chop the shallot and soften it gently in 1 oz/25 g of butter, without browning. Drain the peas, add them to the shallot and let them absorb the flavour for a few moments, then moisten them with the boiling broth, cover and let simmer until the liquid has been almost entirely absorbed.

Meanwhile cook the pasta in plenty of salted boiling water and, while it cooks, purée the tomato sauce. Taste it and, if necessary, adjust the salt and pepper to taste. Drain the pasta when it is *al dente* and sprinkle it with 2 tablespoons of olive oil. Season it with the tomato sauce and the peas, mixing carefully. Sprinkle with chopped parsley and serve it with the grated cheese.

Pasta Shells with Four Cheeses

Lumaconi ai 4 Formaggi

To serve 1

1 oz/25 g Parmesan cheese

1 oz/25 g Sbrinz cheese

1 oz/25 g Emmental cheese

1 oz/25 g Fontina cheese

butter

4 tablespoons/60 ml milk

nutmeg

1 egg yolk

4 oz/100 g pasta shells (lumaconi)

a little chopped parsley for garnish

Preparation and cooking time: about 30 minutes
Grate the Parmesan and Sbrinz cheeses. Cut the Emmental and Fontina cheeses into small cubes and mix these 2 cheeses together well.

In a saucepan melt 1 oz/25 g of butter, without browning; remove the saucepan from the heat and add the 4 cheeses, stirring vigorously with a small wooden spoon. Place the saucepan again over a very low heat (or in a *bain-marie*) and, stirring constantly, melt the cheeses slightly. Then add the warm milk in a trickle, mixing constantly until thoroughly smooth and blended, then season it with a grating of nutmeg. Take off the heat and add a fresh egg yolk. Keep the sauce warm in a *bain-marie,* stirring often.

Cook the pasta in salted boiling water with the pan uncovered, until *al dente.* Drain, pour the cheese "fondue" over it and sprinkle with a pinch of finely chopped parsley. Serve at once before the cheese mixture becomes firm.

Delicate Polenta with Mushrooms

Polenta Delicata ai Funghi

To serve 4

1½ pints/900 ml milk

8 oz/250 g corn meal

4 oz/100 g semolina

¾-1 lb/400 g small mushrooms (preferably ceps)

3 oz/75 g butter

flour

ground nutmeg

scant 4 oz/100 g grated Emmental cheese

2 egg yolks

1 garlic clove

a handful of parsley

olive oil

thyme

Preparation and cooking time: about 1 hour
Place on the heat a large saucepan containing 1 pint/500 ml of water and 1½ pints/750 ml of the milk and slowly bring to the boil. Mix the corn meal with the semolina. As soon as the liquids start to boil add the salt and, after a few moments, sprinkle in the mixed corn meal and semolina gradually. At the beginning stir with a small whisk, then with a wooden spoon. Cook the polenta over a medium heat for about 40 minutes, stirring frequently.

In the meantime, clean the mushrooms, trim the stems and wipe the mushrooms with a damp cloth, then cut them into thin slices. In a small saucepan melt 1 oz/25 g of the butter, add the flour and stir with a wooden spoon to prevent lumps forming. Moisten with ¼ pint/150 ml of boiling milk poured in a trickle and, stiring constantly, bring the sauce to the boil.

Remove from the heat, season with salt and ground nutmeg, then stir in the Emmental cheese and 2 egg yolks, stirring vigorously after each addition. Keep the sauce warm in a *bain-marie,* stirring it once in a while.

Finely chop a garlic clove together with a handful of parsley; soften the mixture in 1 oz/25 g of butter and 2 tablespoons of oil, without browning. Add the mushrooms and leave for not more than 5 minutes, seasoning with salt and pepper and a pinch of thyme.

Remove the polenta from the heat and fold in the remaining butter softened and cut in small pieces, then pour it on to a round serving board and make a hollow in the center; pour in the cheese sauce, spread over the mushroom slices and sprinkle with a little chopped parsley. Serve at once.

Pasta and Chick Peas
Pasta e Ceci

To serve 6

4 oz/100 g dried chick peas

1 medium onion

1 large garlic clove

1 small carrot

1 stick celery

8 fresh sorrel leaves

½ sprig of rosemary

4 oz/100 g peeled tomatoes

2 large potatoes, together weighing about 12 oz/350 g

olive oil

2 stock cubes

4 oz/100 g pasta

3 tablespoons grated Parmesan cheese

Preparation and cooking time: 2½ hours plus overnight soaking

Soak the chick peas overnight in cold water. The following day, finely chop the onion with the garlic, carrot and celery together with the sorrel and rosemary leaves. Drain the chick peas and put in a saucepan with all the other ingredients. Chop the tomatoes finely and add these, along with the whole peeled potatoes. Pour in 3½ pints/2 litres of cold water and 3 tablespoons of olive oil. Crumble in the stock cubes and bring to the boil. Then turn the heat down to the minimum, cover the pan and simmer for about 2 hours, stirring from time to time.

Remove the potatoes with a slotted spoon and purée them with about a third of the chick peas, returning the purée to the saucepan. Bring back to the boil and pour in the pasta. Boil over a fairly high heat, keeping the pan uncovered and stirring from time to time. Taste and add salt if required, then stir in 3 tablespoons of olive oil and the Parmesan cheese. Add a little freshly ground pepper. Stir and serve at once.

Pasta Tubes with Broccoli
Sedanini con Broccoletti

To serve 4

1¾ lb/800 g young broccoli

4-6 shallots

a little parsley

2 sprigs fresh fennel

olive oil

12 oz/350 g small pasta tubes

grated Pecorino cheese

Preparation and cooking time: about 30 minutes

Wash the broccoli and divide it into flowerets. Chop the stalks into lengths of about 1½-2 inches/4-5 cm. Cook the broccoli in a saucepan of boiling water for 7-8 minutes. Leave uncovered. While the broccoli is cooking, finely slice the shallots. Chop the parsley and fennel together and sauté with the shallots in 5 tablespoons of olive oil.

Remove the broccoli from the pan with a slotted spoon and, without draining too thoroughly, place it in the frying pan with the other ingredients. Fry the broccoli in turn without mixing – simply shake the pan. Add freshly ground pepper. Into the same water used for the broccoli, there should be at least 5 pints/3 litres, pour the sedanini and boil until the pasta is cooked *al dente*. Drain and sauté in the pan with the broccoli, sprinkling with the Pecorino cheese. Serve at once.

Pasta with broccoli

Garlic, Oil and Hot Pepper Sauce for Long, Hollow Macaroni

Aglio, Olio e Peperoncino per Fusilli Lunghi Bucati

6 garlic cloves

2 hot chilli peppers

1 lb/500 g hollow macaroni

olive oil

2 oz/50 g grated Parmesan cheese

2 oz/50 g grated Pecorino cheese

Chop the garlic and chilli peppers coarsely and liquidize them with ¼ pint/150 ml of cold water. Add this to a panful of salted hot water, bring to the boil and simmer for 15 minutes, then strain into a second pan. Boil the pasta in this and, when it is cooked *al dente,* drain it and add ⅓ pint/200 ml of olive oil and the two cheeses, stirring well.

Pasta Quills with Yellow Pepper Sauce

Mezze Penne al Peperone

To serve 4

1 large yellow pepper

1 medium onion

olive oil

1 garlic clove

5-6 fresh mint leaves

4 fresh basil leaves

8 oz/250 g skinned tomatoes

½ pint/250 ml light stock (or use a stock cube)

12 oz/350 g small pasta quills (mezze penne)

2 tablespoons grated Pecorino cheese

Preparation and cooking time: 1¼ hours

Grill and peel a ripe, yellow pepper, then cut it into 1 inch/2 cm cubes. Finely slice the onion and soften with the pepper cubes in 5 tablespoons of olive oil, taking care not to brown any of the ingredients. Then add a large garlic clove, with the green core removed, 5-6 leaves of fresh mint and 4 fresh basil leaves, all finely chopped.

Stir, and fry slowly for a few minutes, then pureé the tomatoes and add them. Add the stock and a little salt and pepper and cook in a partly covered pan for about 35 minutes, when the sauce will be just about reduced and well-cooked. Purée half the sauce and return to the pan containing the remainder. Mix well together.

Cook the pasta in salted boiling water until *al dente*. Drain, add a tablespoon of olive oil, then the prepared sauce and the grated Pecorino cheese. Stir and serve.

Pasta with yellow pepper sauce

Basil Sauce for Pasta Caps

Sugo al Basilico per Orecchiette

5-6 fresh basil leaves

1 garlic clove

2 oz/50 g cooking fat or butter

olive oil

12 oz/350 g pasta caps (orecchiette)

2 tablespoons grated Parmesan cheese

1 tablespoon grated Pecorino cheese

Wash the basil and chop it with the garlic. Heat the fat and 3 tablespoons of olive oil and fry the basil and garlic very gently, adding a generous quantity of freshly ground pepper. Cook and drain the pasta, tip it into the sauce and sprinkle with the two cheeses before serving.

Pasta with Lentils

Pasta e Lenticche

To serve 6

8 oz/250 g dried lentils

6 oz/150 g potatoes

2 sage leaves

1 large garlic clove

a little parsley

4 oz/100 g peeled tomatoes

olive oil

2 stock cubes

4 oz/100 g pasta shells

3 tablespoons grated Parmesan cheese

Preparation and cooking time: 2½ hours

Pick over the lentils to make sure there are no impurities or grit. Wash under warm running water and place in a saucepan. Peel and dice the potatoes and put these in too. Chop the sage, garlic and parsley and add these too. Purée the tomatoes and add these together with 3 tablespoons of olive oil. Stir and pour in 3½ pints/2 litres of cold water and bring to the boil. Turn the heat down to the minimum as soon as the mixture starts to boil, add the stock cubes, cover and simmer for about 2 hours, stirring from time to time.

When the cooking is completed, purée a ladleful of the mixture and return the purée to the pan.

Stir in and bring back to the boil. Then add the pasta, stir and cook until the pasta is *al dente*. Remove from the heat, add a little freshly milled pepper, 3 tablespoons of olive oil and the Parmesan cheese. Serve, and sprinkle each portion with chopped parsley.

Pasta Ribbons with Mushrooms

Fettuccia Riccia ai Funghi

To serve 1

1 thick slice onion

a few fresh sprigs of parsley

1 garlic clove

butter

1 cep mushroom

1 tablespoon dry Marsala wine

¼ stock cube

½ teaspoon cornflour

milk

4 oz/100 g scalloped pasta ribbons (fettuccia)

Preparation and cooking time: about 30 minutes

Finely chop together the onion, a few parsley sprigs and a small garlic clove. Soften in 1 oz/25 g butter, melted in a small pan. Meanwhile, scrape the dirt from the stem of a very fresh, firm cep mushroom and wash or wipe the cap with a damp cloth. Slice thinly and add the slices to the onion mixture. Sauté for a few minutes, stirring gently with a wooden spoon.

Next, moisten with the dry Marsala wine and season with a quarter of a stock cube. Dissolve half a teaspoon of cornflour in 2 tablespoons of cold milk and add it to the slices of mushroom, stirring with a wooden spoon. Leave the sauce on a very low heat for 4-5 minutes.

Cook the pasta until *al dente* in plenty of salted boiling water. Drain, and pour over the mushrooms sauce to which you have added, at the last moment, half a teaspoon of chopped parsley.

Pasta ribbons with mushrooms

Mushroom Pizza
Pizza ai Funghi

To serve 4

12 oz/350 g mushrooms

juice of 1 lemon

olive oil

1 garlic clove

flour

14 oz/400 g bread dough

a little chopped parsley

Preparation and cooking time: 45 minutes

Pre-heat the oven to 400-425°F/ 200-220°C/gas mark 6-7. Peel or wipe the mushrooms and trim the stalks. As they are ready, put them in a bowl of cold water to which the lemon juice has been added. Heat 3 tablespoons of olive oil in a frying pan. Crush the garlic and put it in the hot olive oil. Fry until the garlic browns and then remove from the frying pan. Slice the mushrooms directly into the hot oil and sauté for 3-4 minutes, seasoning with salt and pepper.

Flour a pastry-board and roll the dough into a ball, then flatten it out to a round about 12 inches/30 cm in diameter. Lightly oil a baking tray and place the dough on it. With your fingertips press down the dough just inside the edge to give it a bigger crust. Spread the mushrooms over the pizza and pour over a trickle of olive oil. Sprinkle with chopped parsley and place in the oven for about 15 minutes. Serve hot from the oven, cut into quarters.

Naples-style Pizza
Pizza alla Napoletana

To serve 1-2

flour

8 oz/250 g pizza dough

olive oil

2-3 fresh or tinned medium tomatoes, skinned

a pinch of oregano

2-3 large fresh basil leaves

1 garlic clove, green shoot removed

Preparation and cooking time: about 30 minutes, plus any defrosting time.

Pre-heat the oven to 400-425°F/ 200-220°C/gas mark 6-7. Flour a pastry-board and roll the dough into a ball, then flatten it out to an 8 inch/20 cm round. Lightly grease a baking tray and place the dough on it. With your fingertips, press down the dough just inside the edge to give it a raised edge.

Chop the tomatoes, season with a little salt and a pinch of oregano and spread over the pizza. Wipe the basil leaves with a damp cloth and finely chop them before sprinkling them over the tomato. Finely chop or slice half a garlic clove and sprinkle this on too. Do not spread these ingredients right to the edges of the dough. Drizzle on plenty of good olive oil and bake for about 12 minutes. Serve straight from the oven on a flat, warmed plate.

Roman-style Pizza
Pizza alla Romana

To serve 1

flour

8 oz/250 g bread or pizza dough

2 fresh medium tomatoes, skinned

3 oz/75 g Mozzarella cheese

a pinch of oregano

3 fresh basil leaves, chopped

2 tablespoons grated Pecorino cheese

olive oil

Preparation and cooking time: 30 minutes plus any defrosting time

Pre-heat the oven to 400-425°F/ 200-220°C/gas mark 6-7. Flour a pastry-board and roll the dough, defrosted if necessary, into a ball, then flatten it out to an 8 inch/20 cm round. Lightly grease a baking tray and place the dough on it. With your fingertips, press down the dough just inside the edge to give it a slightly raised edge.

Remove the seeds from the tomatoes and slice finely. Spread over the pizza. Lightly sprinkle with salt and pepper, a pinch of oregano and the basil. Sprinkle the Pecorino on top and pour over a thin trickle of olive oil. Bake in the oven for 12-14 minutes until the pizza is golden brown. Pour over a thin trickle of oil before serving hot.

Roman-style pizza

Tortelloni with Courgettes
Tortelloni di Zucchini

To serve 6

1 lb/500 g courgettes

12 oz/350 g tomatoes

1 oz/30 g plain flour

4 oz/125 g button mushrooms

2 oz/60 g butter

4 oz/125 g grated Parmesan cheese

5 eggs

fresh basil

garlic

dried marjoram

olive oil

nutmeg

Preparation and cooking time: 2 hours

1) Clean and dice the courgettes. Clean and slice the mushrooms. Heat ¼ pint/150 ml of oil in large frying pan with a garlic clove (to be removed before brown). Add the mushrooms and the courgettes and cook for 20 minutes. Allow to cool and then blend them with a food processor. Stir in the Parmesan, 2 egg yolks, a sprinkle of marjoram, a level tablespoon of flour, a sprinkle of nutmeg and salt and pepper.

2) Mix the remaining flour with salt and 3 eggs, and work into a dough. Roll thinly and cut into 2 inch/5 cm strips.

3) Cut the strips into 2 inch/5 cm squares. Put a teaspoon of the courgette mixture onto each square.

4) Fold the tortelloni into triangles, and firmly seal the edges with your fingertips.

5) Peel and dice the tomatoes, melt the butter in a large fry pan and add the tomatoes, salt and 7 chopped basil leaves (or 1 teaspoon dry basil).

6) Cook the sauce for 5 minutes. Meanwhile bring to the boil a large pan of salted water. Drop in the tortelloni. Drain them when still underdone (*al dente*) and add to the sauce. Cook together for a few minutes.

Transfer to a soup tureen and serve hot.

1

2

3

4

5

6

SIDE DISHES

Throughout Italy vegetables are usually in plentiful supply and are comparatively cheap, with a wide seasonal variety available from region to region. As a result, vegetables form an important part of a meal and are often served as a separate course. With their own accompaniments and sauces, they are ideal as an imaginative side dish or main course. Recipes with rice, eggs and cheese are also widely enjoyed. If the recommended Italian cheeses are hard to find, then use an equivalent soft, hard or blue cheese instead.

& MAIN COURSES

Cheese and Fennel Salad

Insalata di Finochi, Composta

To serve 4-5

2 fennel bulbs

a few drops lemon juice

½ garlic clove

3 oz/75 g Emmental cheese

1 teaspoon mustard

1 tablespoon white wine vinegar

olive oil

1 chive

Preparation time: about 40 minutes

Clean the fennel bulbs, removing the green leaves, small shoots and the first layer, then cut them in half and place them in cold water with a few drops of lemon juice added.

Meanwhile rub the inside of a salad bowl with half a garlic clove. Cut the cheese into very thin slices and place in the salad bowl. Put a pinch of salt, a grinding of white pepper, a teaspoon of mustard and a tablespoon of white wine vinegar into a small bowl; stir with a fork until the salt has dissolved, then dilute with 4 tablespoons of olive oil and mix the ingredients well.

Drain the pieces of fennel well, dry them, cut them in thin slices and add to the cheese, also add the chopped chive, and toss gently. Pour over the prepared dressing and toss again.

Vegetarian Pasta Salad

Conchiglie Vegetariane

To serve 8

4 oz/100 g fresh peas

2 baby carrots

1 lb/500 g fluted pasta shells

4 oz/100 g tinned sweetcorn

2 tablespoons mustard

juice of ½ lemon

olive oil

Preparation and cooking time: about 45 minutes

Heat 2 saucepans of water (one large one and one slightly smaller) and salt them both when they come to the boil. Cook the fresh shelled peas in the smaller pan, boiling them for about 15 minutes. Drain well, reserving the water, and leave to dry on kitchen paper. Trim and dice the carrots and cook them in the same water for about 12 minutes. Drain and mix with the peas.

Cook the fluted pasta shells in the larger saucepan of boiling water. Drain the pasta when it is cooked *al dente*, and spread it out on a tray to cool.

Drain the sweetcorn and mix it in a salad bowl with the cold peas and carrots. Prepare the dressing: place the mustard, the juice of half a lemon and a pinch of salt and pepper in a bowl. Beat the mixture and blend in 6 tablespoons of olive oil.

Mix the pasta with the vegetables in the salad bowl and dress with the prepared sauce. Stir well and serve.

Cheese and fennel salad

Carrot and Walnut Fritters

Frittelline di Carote e Noci

To serve 4

1 lb/500 g baby carrots

2 oz/50 g flour

2 oz/50 g butter

1 egg

2 oz/50 g walnuts, coarsely chopped

oil for frying

Preparation and cooking time: about 40 minutes

Cook the carrots in salted boiling water until tender. Drain and cool on kitchen paper. Purée the carrots in a liquidizer and dry out the purée in a pan on a low heat if it seems too liquid. Stir in the flour and season with a pinch of salt and pepper. Stir in the melted butter and the egg yolk.

Beat the egg white until stiff and fold it gently into the carrot mixture. Add the walnuts. The mixture should be soft and slightly sticky. Divide the mixture into fritters about the size of a walnut.

Heat plenty of oil in a large frying pan and cook the fritters on a moderate heat. Turn the fritters during cooking so that they brown on all sides. Drain on kitchen paper and keep warm. Arrange on a warmed plate and serve hot.

Vegetarian pasta salad

Bean Sprouts with Parmesan

Germogli di Soia alla Parmigiana

To serve 4

12 oz/350 g bean sprouts

2 oz/50 g butter

1 garlic clove

½ stock cube

grated Parmesan cheese

Preparation and cooking time: about 30 minutes

Pre-heat the oven to 400°F/200°C/gas mark 6. Heat a large saucepanful of water and add a little salt when it begins to boil. Wash the bean sprouts thoroughly under cold running water, then drain and put into the boiling water for about 1 minute. Remove with a slotted spoon, place in a colander and leave to drain thoroughly.

Heat the butter in a large frying pan and put in a lightly crushed garlic clove. Once this is brown, remove it. Now put in the bean sprouts and crumble in the half stock cube. Mix carefully and fry gently for a few minutes. Arrange in an ovenproof dish in layers, sprinkling a little Parmesan cheese and grinding a little fresh pepper over each layer. Cook in the oven for about 10 minutes, then serve.

Sweet Peppers with Scrambled Egg

Peperoni e Uova

To serve 4

1 yellow and 1 red pepper, together weighing about 1 lb/500 g

8 oz/250 g firm, ripe tomatoes

3-4 large fresh basil leaves

olive oil

1 garlic clove

2 eggs

1 teaspoon grated Pecorino cheese

Preparation and cooking time: about 45 minutes

Wash and dry the peppers and cut them in half lengthwise, discarding the stalks and seeds. Cut them again lengthwise into strips about ¾ inch/2 cm wide.

Parboil the tomatoes in lightly salted water. Skin them and cut them in half, discarding the seeds. Chop into small pieces. Wipe the basil leaves with a damp cloth.

Heat 4 tablespoons of olive oil and the lightly crushed garlic clove in a frying pan. Discard the garlic as soon as it has browned. Fry the peppers gently until tender (about 15 minutes), stirring occasionally during cooking. Stir in the tomatoes and basil leaves and season with a little salt and pepper. Cook on a low heat for a further 15 minutes, adding a little boiling water if the mixture becomes too dry.

Beat the eggs with a pinch of salt and pepper and stir them into the vegetables. Keep stirring until the eggs have scrambled. Remove from the heat and serve sprinkled with the grated Pecorino cheese.

Stuffed baked aubergines (below) *and* *peppers with scrambled eggs* (bottom)

Stuffed Baked Aubergines

Melanzane dello Skipper

To serve 4

2 large aubergines, together weighing about 1½ lb/750 g

1 small onion

2-3 fresh basil leaves

1 garlic clove

olive oil

8 oz/250 g firm ripe tomatoes

½ stock cube

4 heaped tablespoons breadcrumbs

1 tablespoon chopped parsley

2 tablespoons grated Pecorino cheese

Preparation and cooking time: about 1¾ hours.

Wash the aubergines and halve them lengthwise. Scoop out the flesh, leaving a border of about ½ inch/1 cm and being careful not to damage the skin. Cut the flesh into small pieces.

Chop the onion and basil and fry gently with a whole garlic clove in 4 tablespoons of olive oil. Stir in the pieces of aubergine and cook for a few minutes.

Chop the tomatoes finely, process them in a blender and add them to the pan. Season with the crumbled half stock cube and a little pepper. Cover the pan and cook on a moderate heat for about 20 minutes, stirring occasionally. Remove from the heat and leave to cool. Discard the garlic. Blend in 3 heaped tablespoons of fresh breadcrumbs, the chopped parsley and grated Pecorino cheese.

Pre-heat the oven to 375°F/190°C/gas mark 5. Stuff the aubergines with the prepared mixture and place them in an oiled ovenproof serving dish. Sprinkle with a tablespoon of breadcrumbs and a little olive oil. Cover the dish with foil and cook in the oven for about 1 hour. Remove the foil after about 45 minutes so that the aubergines can brown slightly on top. Serve either hot or cold.

Baby Onions and Grapes with Marsala Wine

Cipollette e Uva al Marsala

To serve 4-5

about 4 dozen green grapes

1¾ lb/800 g baby onions

butter

1 garlic clove

1 bay leaf

6 tablespoons/100 ml dry Marsala wine

granulated sugar

1 tablespoon white wine vinegar

½ stock cube

½ teaspoon cornflour

Preparation and cooking time: about 1¼ hours

Peel the grapes carefully, using a knife with a short, thin blade. Remove the outer skin and any imperfections from the onions, wash them, then plunge them into salted boiling water and boil them for about 10 minutes.

In the meantime melt a large knob of butter in a frying pan and add the slightly crushed garlic clove and a small bay leaf. Next add the well-drained onions and brown them lightly, moving the pan continuously. Moisten with the Marsala wine, add a good pinch of sugar and the vinegar and flavour with the crumbled half stock cube.

Cover and let the liquid reduce by about half then remove the garlic and bay leaf, add the grapes and half a teaspoon of cornflour dissolved in 2 tablespoons of cold water. Stir gently and keep the preparation on a rather high heat until the liquid has thickened and formed a dense sauce. At this point pour the onions and grapes into a deep serving dish and serve at once.

Mediterranean Courgettes

Zucchini Mediterranea

To serve 4

¾-1 lb/350 g small tender courgettes

2-3 sprigs fresh parsley

capers

1 garlic clove

oregano

olive oil

Preparation and cooking time: about 30 minutes

Boil a large saucepanful of salted water. Trim the courgettes and cut into lengths of about 2 inches/5 cm. Cut each piece vertically in half and then into small sticks. Put the courgettes into the boiling water and boil for a few minutes until they are cooked but still firm. Remove with a slotted spoon and lay them to cool on kitchen paper.

Trim and wash the parsley, then dry with a clean cloth. Drain the capers and peel a small garlic clove. Coarsely chop these ingredients together and put in a bowl. Season with a pinch of salt and a small pinch of freshly ground pepper and flavour with a pinch of dried oregano. Pour in 6 tablespoons of olive oil and mix well. Arrange the cold courgettes on a small serving dish and pour over the dressing, mixing the salad at the table. This tasty and light vegetable dish may be served with a wide variety of meals.

Grandma's chick peas (top) and *Mediterranean courgettes*

Grandma's Chick Peas

Ceci Della Nonna

To serve 4

8 oz/250 g tinned chick peas

olive oil

2 small tomatoes, skinned

½ stock cube

1 small green pimiento

1 small onion

Preparation and cooking time: about 30 minutes

Rinse the chick peas thoroughly under warm running water, then leave to drain. Heat 2 tablespoons of olive oil in a frying pan and as soon as it is hot, put in the tomatoes, breaking them coarsely with a fork. Crumble in the half stock cube and fry over a low heat until some of the liquid from the tomatoes has evaporated.

Meanwhile, drain the pimiento and cut into strips no longer than ½ inch/1 cm. Slice the onion into fine rings, beginning at the centre where it is widest and using a very sharp knife. Add the chick peas and pimiento to the tomatoes and fry for a few minutes, so that the chick peas are just heated up. Then turn the mixture into a bowl and arrange the onion rings on top. Sprinkle with freshly ground pepper and serve.

Braised Brussels Sprouts

Cavolini di Bruxelles, Stufati

To serve 6

2¼ lb/1 kg Brussels sprouts

4 oz/100 g butter

juice of 1 lemon

grated Parmesan cheese

Preparation and cooking time: about 1¼ hours

Pre-heat the oven to 350°F/180°C/gas mark 4. Remove the tough outer leaves from the Brussels sprouts and trim the stalks. Cut each one into quarters and leave to soak in a large bowl of lightly salted cold water for about 30 minutes. Drain well and arrange in a buttered, fairly heavy, ovenproof dish which can also be used as a serving dish. Dot the rest of the butter among the Brussels sprouts. Sprinkle with salt and pepper and pour over the strained lemon juice.

Cover the dish with a tightly fitting lid and cook in the oven for about 30 minutes or a little longer, depending on the size and freshness of the sprouts. From time to time turn the sprouts over then replace the lid. The Brussels sprouts should end up perfectly cooked and dry. Remove from the oven, sprinkle with a tablespoon of Parmesan, mix with care and serve.

Ring of Spinach

Corona di Spinaci

To serve 6

salt

1¼ lb/600 g frozen spinach

1 small onion

3 oz/75 g butter

4 eggs

6 tablespoons/100 ml milk

nutmeg

2 oz/50 g grated Parmesan cheese

breadcrumbs

Preparation and cooking time: about 1 hour

In a saucepan bring a small amount of water to the boil, salt it, then plunge in the frozen spinach and cook until defrosted. Drain, rinse under cold running water and squeeze well. Chop the onion and soften it in 2 oz/50 g of the butter, melted in a large frying pan. Finely chop the spinach and cook with the onions for a few minutes then remove from the heat to a bowl to cool completely. Pre-heat the oven to 350°F/180°C/gas mark 4.

In another bowl beat the eggs with the milk, season with salt and pepper and a good pinch of nutmeg. Add the egg mixture and the grated Parmesan cheese to the spinach. Adjust the salt to taste, then pour the mixture into a ring mould, well buttered and sprinkled with breadcrumbs, about 1¾ pints/1 litre in capacity and 9 inches/23 cm in diameter.

Put the mould in the pre-heated oven for about 30 minutes. Rest it for 5 minutes before turning out on to a warmed serving dish. Serve garnished, if you like, with fresh tomato sauce.

Ring of spinach

Crêpes with Mushrooms and Artichokes

Crespelle con Funghi e Carciofi

To make 16 crêpes

3 artichokes

juice of ½ lemon

1 medium onion

1 garlic clove

a few sprigs parsley

4 oz/100 g butter

olive oil

6 oz/150 g mushrooms, cleaned

¼ pint/150 ml stock (or use a stock cube)

dried thyme

6 oz/150 g flour

1¼ pints/750 ml milk

nutmeg

2 eggs and 1 egg white

3 oz/75 g grated Parmesan cheese

Preparation and cooking time: about 2 hours

Clean the artichokes and put them in a bowl of cold water with the juice of half a lemon. Finely chop the onion with a garlic clove and a few sprigs of parsley and fry in knob of butter and 2 tablespoons of olive oil. Drain the artichokes and chop, cut up the mushrooms and add both to the pan. Stir and leave for a few minutes. Then pour in the stock, add a little salt, pepper and a pinch of thyme.

Cover and simmer over a medium heat for about 30 minutes, until the mushrooms and artichokes are tender and the liquid has almost entirely evaporated.

Purée the contents of the pan. Make a thick béchamel sauce with 1½ oz/40 g butter, the same amount of flour and a scant ½ pint/250 ml of milk. Season with salt and nutmeg. Add this to the mushroom and artichoke purée, together with an egg yolk and 2 oz/50 g

Parmesan cheese. Taste and add salt if necessary.

Now make the crêpes: beat the 2 whole eggs and the egg white in a bowl, sift in 4 oz/100 g flour and add a pinch of salt. Dilute with ½ pint/300 ml of milk beating with a whisk to prevent lumps forming. Brush the bottom of a frying pan with a little oil and heat it well. Pour in a ladleful of the crêpe batter and shake the pan rapidly to spread it evenly over the bottom of the pan. Slowly cook one side until it is golden then toss and brown the other side. Turn on to a plate and continue to make 15 more crêpes. Spread them with the mushroom and artichoke mixture and fold them over. Pre-heat the oven to 400°F/200°C/gas mark 6.

Prepare a béchamel sauce with 1 oz/25 g each of butter and flour and the rest of the milk, and when it is boiling, pour it into a round dish about 11 inches/28 cm in diameter, spreading it evenly. Arrange the crêpes in the dish, pour over the rest of the butter, melted, and sprinkle with the remaining grated Parmesan cheese. Bake in the oven for about 15 minutes, then serve.

Peppers and potatoes

Spinach Pie with Olives
Spinacina alle Olive

To serve 6-8

1 lb/500 g spinach

2 oz/50 g butter

1 oz/25 g flour

¼ pint/150 ml milk

1 oz/25 g grated Parmesan cheese

4 oz/100 g puff pastry

2 eggs, lightly beaten

ground nutmeg

1 tablespoon breadcrumbs

4 walnuts, chopped

2 slices Piccadolce cheese, diced

Preparation and cooking time: about 1 hour plus any thawing time

Chop the spinach and sauté in 1 oz/25 g of butter. Cook briskly until the moisture has evaporated and then place in a bowl. Prepare a béchamel sauce with a knob of butter, the flour and the milk. Stir the spinach and Parmesan cheese into the sauce and leave to cool.

Meanwhile defrost the pastry if necessary, roll out thinly and use to line a greased 8 inch/20 cm square baking pan.

Stir the eggs into the béchamel sauce and season with salt, pepper and a little ground nutmeg. Prick the pastry with a fork and sprinkle with the breadcrumbs.

Pre-heat the oven to 375°F/190°C/ gas mark 5. Pour half the prepared mixture into the pan, sprinkle with the chopped walnuts and cover with the rest of the sauce. Trim off any excess pastry. Bake the pie in the bottom of the oven for 35-40 minutes. Sprinkle the pie with the diced Piccadolce cheese and cook for a further 5 minutes or until the cheese has melted. Turn on to a plate and serve immediately.

Peppers and Potatoes
Peperoni e Patate 'Minuetto'

To serve 4-5

2 potatoes of equal size, together weighing about 12 oz/350 g

2 red peppers

5 oz/150 g onions

1 large garlic clove

4 basil leaves

olive oil

a little stock (or use stock cube)

a little chopped parsley

Preparation and cooking time: about 1 hour

Peel the potatoes, wash them and cut them in slices about ¼ inch/5 mm thick. Cut each slice with a round, smooth pastry cutter about 1½ inches/4 cm in diameter.

Heat salted water in a small saucepan; as soon as it starts to boil plunge in the potato discs and boil for 3-4 minutes, then drain them with a slotted spoon and lay them to dry and cool on a tray covered with a double sheet of kitchen paper. Wash and dry the peppers, cut them in half and clean them; divide each half into 3 strips.

Slice the onions and a large garlic clove very thinly; finely chop the basil leaves. Heat 5 tablespoons of olive oil in a pan, and soften the garlic and onion, without browning them. Next add the pieces of pepper and, after 5 minutes, the potato discs. Lightly fry the vegetables, adding salt, pepper and the basil. Once in a while moisten with a little hot stock. When the potatoes and peppers are cooked and tender (they will take about 25 minutes) arrange the mixture on a serving plate, sprinkle with the chopped parsley and serve immediately.

Braised Baby Onions with Runner Beans
Cipollette e Fagiolini Brasati

To serve 4

8 oz/250 g runner beans

14 oz/400 g baby onions

2 oz/50 g butter

½ stock cube

marjoram

Preparation and cooking time: about 1¼ hours

Trim the beans and wash well, and do the same with the baby onions. Chop them both into 1¼-inch/3 cm pieces. Melt the butter, add the vegetables and sauté them, taking care they do not brown. Salt sparingly, add pepper, and flavour with the crumbled half stock cube and a pinch of marjoram. Stir well with a wooden spoon, add ⅓ pint/200 ml of boiling water and bring back to the boil.

Lower the heat, cover the pan and cook for about 45 minutes or until the vegetables have absorbed all the liquid and are tender and well flavoured. If any liquid remains, raise the heat to dry it off. Turn into a heated vegetable dish and serve at once.

Spinach pie with olives

Stewed Leeks

Porri Stufati

To serve 4

4 large fresh leeks

1 small onion

olive oil

2 tomatoes, peeled and cut into small pieces

6 tablespoons/100 ml light stock (or use stock cube)

Preparation and cooking time: about 50 minutes

Top and tail the leeks, discard the outer leaves and cut in half lengthwise. Finely slice the onions and fry gently in 3 tablespoons of olive oil until transparent. Add the leeks, turning them gently until coated in the oil. Stir in the tomatoes. Pour on the stock and simmer on a low heat for about 40 minutes or until the leeks are tender. Turn the leeks occasionally during cooking and add a little more stock if necessary. Adjust the seasoning to taste.

Carefully place the leeks and onions in a serving dish and cover with the cooking liquid. Serve hot as an accompaniment to red or white meat.

Asparagus in Batter

Asparagi in Pastella, Fritti

To serve 6

3-3½ lb/1.5 kg fresh asparagus

4 oz/100 g flour

1 egg yolk

⅓ pint/200 ml fresh light cream

5 egg whites

oil for frying

Preparation and cooking time: about 1 hour

Peel and tail the asparagus and tie into a bundle with kitchen string. Stand the bundle upright in a saucepan containing a little salted boiling water and cook for about 15 minutes or until tender. Remove the string and spread the asparagus out to dry on kitchen paper.

Meanwhile prepare the batter: sift the flour into a bowl and add the egg yolk and a little salt. Gradually blend in the cream, stirring with a whisk. Beat the egg whites with a pinch of salt until stiff and then fold them into the batter mixture.

Cut the asparagus pieces in half, dip them in the batter and fry them in the hot oil until golden brown. Drain the asparagus on kitchen paper, arrange on a plate and sprinkle with salt. Serve immediately while still hot and crisp.

Treviso-style Grilled Radicchio

Radicchio all'Uso Trevisano

To serve 4

1¾ lb/800 g radicchio

olive oil

black peppercorns

Preparation and cooking time: about 20 minutes

Remove the roots and any damaged leaves from the radicchio heads which should all be about the same size. Wash the heads one at a time under running water and drain thoroughly. Dry with a cloth and divide them in half, or into 4 if they are very big, lengthwise.

Wrap them in the cloth again and squeeze gently to remove any water that may still be inside. Then brush every surface with olive oil and season with salt and freshly ground black pepper. Heat the grill, then place the radicchio halves under it, at a fairly high temperature. Turn them over two or three times with a spatula. If possible, cook on a barbecue over glowing embers, and in this case, turn more frequently.

When the radicchio is cooked and crunchy, remove from the grill, arrange on a heated oval serving dish and serve at once. You can also cook the radicchio in an iron frying pan. For a more delicate flavour heat butter as well as olive oil in the pan, and cook with the lid on.

Haricot Beans with Onion Sauce

Bianchi di Spagna con Salsa di Cipolla

To serve 4

14 oz/400 g tinned haricot beans

1 small onion

butter

1 teaspoon cornflour

3 tablespoons/50 ml milk

10 capers

sprig fresh parsley

Preparation and cooking time: about 30 minutes

Rinse the beans thoroughly under warm running water and drain. Chop the onion almost to a paste. Melt 1 oz/25 g butter in a small saucepan and fry the onion without browning over a low heat for about 15 minutes. Add a tablespoon of warm water, if necessary, to keep the onion soft and to stop it drying out. Sprinkle the cornflour over the onion and blend in well. Dilute gradually with the cold milk to obtain a smooth, consistent sauce. Season with a pinch of salt and simmer over a low heat, stirring constantly, for 5-6 minutes. Remove from the heat and blend at maximum speed until the sauce is completely smooth, then put it in a bowl.

Drain the capers thoroughly, chop them coarsely and add to the chopped parsley. Pour the beans into a serving dish and pour over the onion sauce. Sprinkle with the chopped parsley and capers and serve. This makes a delicate accompaniment to boiled meat dishes.

Haricot beans with onion sauce (above right) and potatoes with herb butter

Potatoes with Herb Butter

Patate al Burro Aromatico

To serve 4

1¼ lb/600 g medium-sized potatoes

butter

ground thyme

nutmeg

1 sprig fresh parsley for garnish

Preparation and cooking time: about 1 hour

Pre-heat the oven to 375°F/190°C/gas mark 5. Peel the potatoes and cut into slices about ¼ inch/5 mm thick, using a knife with a serrated blade to give them a scalloped surface. Rinse under cold running water to eliminate most of the excess starch. Heat a large saucepanful of water and add salt when it begins to boil. Put in the potatoes and bring back to the boil, then simmer for about 10 minutes until they just begin to soften.

Meanwhile, prepare the herb butter: soften 1 oz/25 g of butter and cut into small knobs and place in a bowl. Cream with a wooden spoon and when you have obtained a smooth cream, combine with a pinch of salt, plenty of freshly ground pepper, a pinch of thyme and a little grated nutmeg. Blend these ingredients thoroughly.

Remove the potatoes from the water with a slotted spoon and lay out to dry on kitchen paper. Grease a round ovenproof dish with half the herb butter, spreading it thickly on the bottom. Arrange the potatoes in it, overlapping them a little. Cover with more slivers of herb butter and bake in the oven for about 30 minutes until the surface is golden brown. Remove the dish from the oven and leave for a couple of minutes. Sprinkle with the chopped parsley and serve.

Butter Beans with Cheese Sauce

Cornetti Gialli con Salsa al Formaggio

To serve 4-6

1¼ lb/600 g butter beans

2 oz/50 g butter

olive oil

flour

⅓ pint/200 ml stock (or use stock cube)

4 tablespoons/60 ml fresh whipping cream

1 egg yolk

1 oz/25 g grated Emmental and Parmesan cheese

ground nutmeg

Preparation and cooking time: about 1 hour

Heat a pan of water. Break off the ends of the beans and wash them thoroughly. As soon as the water is boiling drop them in and cook for about 20 minutes; they should be very tender. Drain them and sauté in a pan with a large knob of the butter and 2 tablespoons of oil, keeping the heat low and the pan covered. Stir occasionally and cook for about 10 minutes.

Meanwhile melt the remaining butter in another pan, fold in ½ oz/15 g of flour and stir to prevent lumps forming; dilute with the hot stock and bring slowly to the boil. Remove the sauce from the heat, stir in the cream beaten with the egg yolk, the grated Emmental and Parmesan cheeses, a little salt and ground nutmeg. Stir well after the addition of each ingredient. Arrange the beans in a shallow dish, pour over the sauce, toss them gently and serve.

These beans make an ideal side dish for delicate main courses such as fillet of sole, veal escalopes, chicken and turkey breasts, roast saddle or medallions of rabbit. French beans can be prepared with the same cheese sauce.

Carrots with Cream

Carote alla Crema di Latte

To serve 4

1¼ lb/600 g carrots

2 shallots

2 oz/50 g butter

¼ pint/150 ml milk

1 teaspoon cornflour

½ stock cube

nutmeg

4 tablespoons single cream

a little parsley

Preparation and cooking time: about 45 minutes

Peel the carrots, wash and drain them well, then cut them into thin sticks about 1½ inches/4 cm long. Cook for about 10 minutes in salted boiling water.

Meanwhile finely chop the shallots and soften, without browning, in the butter, melted in a large frying pan. Remove the carrot sticks with a slotted spoon and drain well, add them to the shallots and sauté them for a few minutes, turning them gently with a spatula.

Dissolve the cornflour in the cold milk then add it to the carrots, pouring it in a trickle and stirring with a wooden spoon. Season the mixture with half a crumbled stock cube and a grinding of nutmeg, then add the cream, stirring carefully.

Leave to simmer for a few minutes on a very low heat, stirring occasionally, until the mixture is creamy. Salt to taste and serve garnished with a few parsley leaves.

Potato Rings

'Bomboloni' di Patate

To serve 10

14 oz/400 g floury potatoes

about 1¼ lb/600 g plain flour

3 eggs

4 oz/100 g butter

1½ oz/40 g dried yeast

a little milk

oil for deep-frying

caster sugar

cinnamon

Preparation and cooking time: about 1 hour plus 1½ hours' rising

Boil the potatoes, then peel them and mash immediately. Sift about 18 oz/500 g of flour, make a well in the centre and add the mashed potato, the whole eggs (not straight from the refrigerator), a pinch of salt and the softened butter, cut in small pieces. Dissolve the yeast in a small cupful of warm milk, add to the other ingredients and work the mixture in well. Dip your hands in flour to prevent the mixture sticking to them as you knead, but do not use too much, to avoid altering the proportions.

As soon as the dough is soft and pliable, cut it into pieces and form them one at a time into long rolls with a diameter of about ¾ inch/2 cm. Cut these into lengths of about 6 inches/15 cm and form them into rings. Place them on 3 or more trays, lined with tea-towels sprinkled lightly with flour, and keep them well spaced, so that they will not stick together when they rise. Cover the small rings with sheets of kitchen paper and leave to rise in a warm place (about 80°F/28°C), away from draughts, for about 1½ hours.

Place a deep-frying pan, fitted with a basket and containing plenty of oil, on the heat and when it is very hot, but not boiling, plunge the rings into it 2 or 3 at a time, turning them several times during cooking. The heat must be kept moderate, otherwise the outside of the rings may brown, while the inside is still uncooked. As soon as they are ready, lift them out of the oil, using a slotted spoon, and drain well, then spread them out on a plate covered with kitchen paper and proceed to cook the others. In a deep plate, mix some caster sugar with a little ground cinnamon and dip the hot rings in this, then serve immediately.

Stuffed Tomatoes

Pomi Dorati con Riso

To serve 4

1 stock cube

4 tomatoes, of equal size, together weighing about 1 lb/500 g

2 oz/50 g butter

1 oz/25 g chopped onion

2 oz/50 g young peas

4 oz/100 g rice

1 tablespoon flour

½ pint/300 ml milk

2 oz/50 g grated Parmesan cheese

fresh basil leaves

Preparation and cooking time: about 1 hour

Pre-heat the oven to 350°F/180°C/gas mark 4. Prepare some stock by heating ½ pint/300 ml of water with half the stock cube. Wash and dry the tomatoes, cut them in half horizontally, sprinkle the insides with a pinch of salt and turn them upside down on a tray covered with kitchen paper. Melt 1 oz/25 g of the butter in an ovenproof dish and put in the onion. Lightly fry, then add the peas and the rice. Then pour in the boiling stock and bring back to the boil. Cover the pan with a lightly buttered sheet of foil and place in the oven for 15 minutes.

Meanwhile, in a small pan prepare a béchamel sauce by melting 1 oz/25 g of butter, stirring in the flour and adding the milk; flavour with the other ½ stock cube and bring to the boil, stirring all the time. Remove the rice from the oven and fluff up with a fork, incorporating a little butter. Leave to cool. Dry the tomatoes with kitchen paper and arrange in a buttered ovenproof dish. Add two-thirds of the béchamel sauce to the rice as well as 1 oz/25 g grated Parmesan cheese. Fill the tomato halves with the mixture, heaping it up to make dome shapes. Pour over the rest of the béchamel and sprinkle over the Parmesan. Place in the oven for about 20 minutes, until the surface of the tomatoes is slightly golden. Serve garnished with fresh basil.

Stuffed tomatoes

Potato and Mushroom Bake

Teglia di Patate e Funghi

To serve 6-8

12 oz/350 g fresh mushrooms

1¾ lb/800 g potatoes, approximately equal in size

a bunch of parsley

3-4 fresh basil leaves

1 large garlic clove

3 tablespoons breadcrumbs

3 tablespoons grated Pecorino cheese

olive oil

Potato and mushroom bake

Preparation and cooking time: about 1½ hours

Pre-heat the oven to 350°F/180°C/gas mark 4. Trim the mushroom stalks and wipe the caps with a damp cloth. Slice them vertically, not too finely. Peel, wash and dry the potatoes, then cut them into slices about ¼ inch/5 mm thick. Wash and dry the parsley and wipe the basil leaves with a damp cloth. Coarsely chop the herbs together with the garlic. Place these ingredients in a bowl and add the breadcrumbs and the Pecorino cheese; season with salt and a little freshly ground pepper. Mix with the fingertips.

Into a round ovenproof dish 10 inches/25 cm in diameter pour 1 tablespoon of olive oil to grease the dish. Make a layer of potato slices, placing them close together without piling them on top of each other. Sprinkle with a pinch of salt and place half the mushrooms on top of the potatoes. Spread half the herb mixture on top. Then pour over 2 tablespoons of olive oil. Make another layer of potatoes and sprinkle with salt. Place

the remaining mushrooms on top and spread the rest of the herb mixture on the mushrooms. Pour 4 tablespoons of olive oil over and cover with foil.

Bake for about 1 hour. Ten minutes before removing from the oven, take off the foil and let the surface brown a little. Remove the pie from the oven and serve.

Savoy Cabbage with Onions

Verza Cipollata

To serve 4

12 oz/350 g savoy cabbage

6 oz/150 g onions

2 oz/50 g cooking fat

rosemary

1 garlic clove

olive oil

1 stock cube

ground nutmeg

a little dry white wine

Preparation and cooking time: about 45 minutes

Bring a large saucepan of water to the boil and add salt. Wash and drain the cabbage and boil for about 5 minutes. Meanwhile slice the onions thinly. Blend the fat with a few leaves of rosemary and a garlic clove and fry gently in 2 tablespoons of olive oil. Add the onions and cook until transparent.

Drain the cabbage, slice thickly and add to the onions. Flavour with half a crumbled stock cube, pepper and a pinch of nutmeg, and sprinkle with a little white wine. Cover the pan and allow the wine to evaporate, stirring occasionally. Test and adjust the seasoning according to taste. Serve immediately.

Bismark-style Leeks

Porro alla Bismarck

To serve 4

16 leeks, not too large and all about the same size

4 oz/125 g butter

2 oz/50 g grated Parmesan cheese

4 eggs

Preparation and cooking time: about 40 minutes

Trim the leeks, removing the roots and the tops of the leaves and discarding the outer layer. Boil water in a narrow saucepan which is deep enough to immerse the white part of the leeks (an asparagus pan is ideal). Add salt when the water begins to boil. Tie the leeks together in bunches of 4 and put them in the boiling water. Boil them for about 10 minutes. Remove them when they are tender but still firm. Untie them and place 4 leeks on each of 4 plates. Melt 2 oz/50 g of the butter and, as soon as it is
hot (it is essential not to let it brown), pour a little over each plate of leeks. Sprinkle with grated Parmesan cheese and keep warm in the lit oven with the door open.

Melt the remaining butter in a large frying pan and break in the eggs. Salt the whites only and cook until the whites have completely set while the yolks remain runny. Remove carefully with a spatula and place an egg in the centre of the white part of the leeks on each plate. Serve at once. This is an ideal accompaniment for very light meat or fish dishes, or it can be served as a course on its own.

Cauliflower with Tomato and Garlic Sauce

Cavolfiore alla Pizzaiola

To serve 6

1 cauliflower weighing about 2 lb/1 kg

1 small onion

2 garlic cloves

olive oil

¾-1 lb/400 g skinned tomatoes

a little sugar

oregano

4 fresh basil leaves

2 oz/50 g butter

4 oz/100 g Mozzarella cheese

grated Parmesan cheese

Preparation and cooking time: about 1 hour

Pre-heat the oven to 400°F/200°C/gas mark 6. Wash the cauliflower thoroughly and simmer in an uncovered pan for about 12 minutes. Meanwhile finely chop the onion and garlic, removing the green centres. Sauté in 4 tablespoons of olive oil and, after a few minutes, add the puréed tomatoes. Add a pinch of sugar and a little salt and pepper. Stir, and cook for about 15 minutes, stirring from time to time. Then add a pinch of oregano and the finely chopped basil leaves.

When the cauliflower is cooked and tender, remove it carefully from the pan with a slotted spoon and place it on a dish covered with a double layer of kitchen paper to absorb the moisture. Then place it in a buttered ovenproof dish with high sides that just contains it. Dice the Mozzarella and scatter the pieces between the cauliflower flowerets. Melt the butter and pour over the cauliflower and sprinkle with grated Parmesan cheese. Place the dish in the oven for about 10 minutes. Pour some of the tomato sauce over the cauliflower and serve immediately, with the remaining sauce served in a sauceboat.

Cauliflower "Ninette"

Cavolfiore "Ninette"

To serve 6

2½ lb/1.5 kg cauliflower

1 small onion

2 oz/50 g small mushrooms

3 oz/75 g butter

olive oil

½ stock cube

6 tablespoons/100 ml whipping cream

1 oz/25 g flour

½ pint/300 ml milk

grated nutmeg

2 or 3 celery leaves

Preparation and cooking time: about 50 minutes

Boil a large saucepanful of salted water. Wash and drain the cauliflower and simmer for about 15 minutes in the uncovered saucepan. While the cauliflower is cooking, finely chop the onion and mushrooms and lightly fry them in 1 oz/25 g of the butter and 1 tablespoon of olive oil, taking care not to let them brown. Crumble in the stock cube and add the cream. Simmer for 2 or 3 minutes, then liquidize in a blender.

Melt the remaining butter in a saucepan and combine with the flour, stirring with a small whisk to prevent lumps forming. Boil the milk and pour in gradually. Bring to the boil, stirring constantly, add salt and a little freshly grated nutmeg. Remove from the heat and stir in the mushroom and onion cream, then pour into a buttered ovenproof dish. Drain the cauliflower thoroughly, divide it into flowerets and arrange in the dish. Place over the heat and simmer gently for a few seconds. Chop the celery leaves and sprinkle over the top before serving.

Cauliflower with tomato and garlic sauce (above left) and *lima beans with mustard*

Lima Beans with Mustard

Fagioli Bianchi alla Senape

To serve 4-6

1½ lb/750 g tinned Lima beans

1 teaspoon white wine vinegar

1 tablespoon mustard

olive oil

1 tablespoon stock

½ garlic clove

a few sprigs parsley

a celery leaf

Preparation time: about 20 minutes

Drain the beans thoroughly and rinse under running water. Then leave them to dry on kitchen paper. In a small bowl, combine a pinch of salt, a pinch of finely ground white pepper, a teaspoon of white wine vinegar and a tablespoon of mustard. Mix with a fork until the salt has dissolved, then add 4 tablespoons of olive oil followed immediately by a tablespoon of boiling stock. Stir vigorously to obtain a smooth sauce. Put the beans in a serving bowl rubbed with garlic and pour the sauce over. Sprinkle with chopped parsley and celery leaf and serve.

Cauliflower Ninette

Mushroom Soufflé

Souffle di Funghi

To serve 4

1 pint/500 ml milk

3 oz/75 g flour

4 oz/100 g butter

2 eggs plus 1 egg yolk

4 tablespoons grated Parmesan cheese

nutmeg

2 oz/50 g Fontina cheese

14 oz/400 g mushrooms

2-3 sprigs fresh parsley

1 medium onion

1 garlic clove

olive oil

½ stock cube

3 tablespoons breadcrumbs

Preparation and cooking time: about 1½ hours

Prepare a thick béchamel sauce with the milk, flour and 2 oz/50 g of the butter. Take it off the heat and add the 3 egg yolks one at a time and the Parmesan. Season. Let it cool.

Wash the mushrooms quickly under running water, dry them and slice them thinly. Finely chop the parsley with the onion and garlic and sauté them in the remaining butter with 1 tablespoon of oil. Add the mushrooms and cook for about 15 minutes. Season with the crumbled half stock cube, remove from the heat and allow to cool. Whisk the 2 egg whites until stiff, add a pinch of salt and fold them gently into the sauce.

Pre-heat the oven to 400°F/200°C/ gas mark 6. Turn a third of the béchamel sauce mixture into a buttered 2½ pint/1.5-litre soufflé dish. Arrange half the mushrooms and a tablespoon of breadcrumbs on top, and cover these with half the remaining mixture, then the remaining mushrooms and another tablespoon of breadcrumbs. Cover the top with the Fontina cheese and breadcrumbs. Cook for about 30 minutes.

Roulades with Cabbage and Spinach

Involtini di Verza con Spinaci

To serve 4

8 large savoy cabbage leaves, together weighing about 1 lb/500 g

8 oz/250 g spinach, boiled and drained

4 oz/100 g butter

4 oz/100 g grated Parmesan cheese

1 small egg

ground nutmeg

Preparation and cooking time: about 1 hour 40 minutes

Bring to the boil a large saucepanful of salted water. Wash the cabbage leaves thoroughly, drain them and boil for about 15 minutes; do not overcook or the leaves may break. Drain, spread them on kitchen paper and leave to cool. Pre-heat the oven to 350°F/180°C/gas mark 4.

Meanwhile prepare the stuffing: Sauté the spinach in 1 oz/25 g of the butter then chop finely and place in a bowl, add 2 oz/50 g of the grated Parmesan cheese, the egg, a pinch of salt, pepper and nutmeg. Mix together well. Divide each cabbage leaf in two, removing the central hard rib. Into each half place a tablespoon of the stuffing, then roll up the leaf enclosing the stuffing inside. Tie each roulade with thread and arrange the roulades in a buttered ovenproof dish. Sprinkle with the remaining grated Parmesan cheese and moisten with the rest of the butter, melting it first.

Bake for about 30 minutes. Serve the roulades, after removing the threads, from the dish in which they were cooked.

Roulades with cabbage and spinach

Mangetout Pie

Sfogliata di Taccole

To serve 6

---

8 oz/250 g puff pastry

---

3 oz/75 g butter

---

12 oz/350 g mangetout

---

1 small onion

---

1 garlic clove

---

1 stock cube

---

grated nutmeg

---

2 oz/50 g grated Parmesan cheese

---

2 eggs

---

1 tablespoon breadcrumbs

---

8 oz/250 g Mozzarella cheese, sliced

Preparation and cooking time: about 1¼ hours plus any thawing time

Defrost the pastry if necessary. Lightly butter a 9 inch/23 cm round ovenproof pie dish.

Trim and wash the mangetout and cook them in salted boiling water for 3-5 minutes. Drain thoroughly.

Finely chop the onion and garlic and fry gently in 2 oz/50 g of the butter until transparent. Add the mangetout and cook over a moderate heat for about 10 minutes, stirring occasionally. Season with the crumbled stock cube, a little pepper and a generous pinch of ground nutmeg.

Turn the mixture out onto a chopping board and chop all the ingredients quite finely. Place in a bowl, mix in the grated Parmesan cheese and the eggs, one at a time. Pre-heat the oven to 375°F/190°C/gas mark 5.

Roll out the pastry to a thickness of about ⅛ inch/3 mm and line the pie dish with it. Sprinkle the base with about a tablespoon of breadcrumbs and pour in the mangetout and egg mixture. Top with slices of Mozzarella cheese.

Bake in the lower part of the oven for about 35 minutes. Remove from the oven and leave to stand for about 10 minutes before serving.

Braised Celery and Fennel

Sedano e Ginocchio

To serve 4

---

12 oz/350 g celery heart

---

1 small leek, white part only

---

4 oz/100 g fennel bulb

---

butter

---

olive oil

---

pepper

---

ground nutmeg

---

2 tablespoons grated Emmental cheese

Preparation and cooking time: about 1 hour

Bring to the boil a large pan of salted water. Cut the celery into pencil-thick pieces 2 inches/5 cm long, removing any strings. Wash thoroughly and boil for about 15 minutes. Meanwhile wash the leek and fennel, and cut the leek into very fine slices and the fennel into wedges. Place them in a pan with a large knob of butter and 2 tablespoons of olive oil and brown them gently, uncovered. Remove the celery from the pan with a slotted spoon and add it to the other vegetables. Stir and continue cooking, still uncovered, adding a little of the celery water from time to time.

Pre-heat the oven to 350°F/180°C gas mark 4. When the vegetables are tender and there is no liquid left season to taste with salt, pepper and ground nutmeg. Place in an ovenproof dish, sprinkle with the cheese and cook in the oven for about 10 minutes. Garnish, if you like, with a few fine fennel leaves and serve immediately.

Mangetout pie

Cheese and Potato Soufflé

Pasticcio di Patate Soufflé

To serve 4

2 lb/1 kg potatoes

¼ pint/150 ml single cream

ground nutmeg

4 oz/100 g grated Gruyère cheese

4 eggs

a little butter

1 tablespoon fresh breadcrumbs

Preparation and cooking time: 1¼ hours
Pre-heat the oven to 350°F/180°C/gas mark 4. Boil the potatoes in salted water. Peel and mash. Stir in the cream and season with salt, pepper and a pinch of nutmeg. Add the grated Gruyère cheese and 4 egg yolks, blending in the yolks one at a time. Whisk the egg whites until stiff and blend into the potato mixture. The mixture should be smooth.

Grease a soufflé dish and sprinkle it with about a tablespoon of fresh breadcrumbs. Pour in the mixture and cook in the pre-heated oven for 15 minutes. Increase the temperature to 400°F/200°C/gas mark 6 and cook for another 10-15 minutes or until the soufflé has risen and is golden brown on top. Serve immediately.

Harlequin Soufflé

Soffiato Arlecchino

To serve 4

½ small red pepper

2 tablespoons vegetable oil

4 oz/100 g butter

½ garlic clove

4 oz/100 g plain flour

1 pint/600 ml milk

ground nutmeg

3 eggs, separated

2 oz/50 g peas, parboiled

4 oz/100 g grated Parmesan cheese

Preparation and cooking time: about 1¼ hours
Cut the pepper into ½ inch/1 cm cubes and sauté for 5 minutes in the vegetable oil and a knob of butter with half a clove of crushed garlic. Drain the pieces of pepper and place them on a plate covered with kitchen paper to absorb the excess oil.

Melt the remaining butter in a pan, stir in the flour and add the milk. Cook gently, stirring to produce a thick béchamel sauce. Season with a pinch of salt, pepper and ground nutmeg. Away from the heat, stir in the 3 egg yolks, one at a time, the pepper cubes, the drained peas and the grated Parmesan cheese, mixing well after each addition. Pre-heat the oven to 375°F/190°C/gas mark 5.

Beat the egg whites to a froth with a pinch of salt and fold them gently into the prepared mixture; pour it into a buttered soufflé dish so that the mixture reaches just over halfway up the sides of the dish. Place in the oven for about 30 minutes; the soufflé should be well risen and brown. Serve immediately.

Ricotta Pie with Peas

Sfogliata di Ricotta ai Piselli

To serve 8

12 oz/300 g puff pastry

a little flour

2 oz/50 g frozen peas

1 lb/500 g Ricotta cheese

3 eggs

3 tablespoons/60 ml milk

2 oz/50 g grated Parmesan cheese

ground nutmeg

2 oz/50 g butter

Preparation and cooking time: about 1 hour plus any defrosting time

Defrost the pastry if necessary, and roll it out on a floured surface. Grease a 10-inch/25 cm pie dish and line it with the pastry.

Pre-heat the oven to 375°F/190°C/gas mark 5. Cook the peas in salted boiling water for 3-4 minutes. Sieve and mash the Ricotta. Blend in the eggs one at a time and then stir in the milk, the grated Parmesan cheese, a little salt and a pinch of ground nutmeg. Blend in 1 oz/25 g of melted butter and the drained peas.

Pour the mixture into the pie shell and cook in the lower part of the oven for about 40 minutes. Turn the pie out on to a plate and serve hot.

Ricotta pie with peas

Golden Aubergine Slices

Melanzane 'Indorate'

To serve 4-5

2 aubergines, each weighing about 12 oz/350 g

2 eggs

white pepper

2 oz/50 g grated Pecorino cheese

6 oz/150 g fresh breadcrumbs

flour

frying oil

Preparation and cooking time: about 40 minutes plus 1 hour's resting

Wash and dry the aubergines and cut them in slices about ½ inch/1 cm thick. Lay them on a large tray covered with kitchen paper and sprinkle them with salt to bring out their bitter juices. Leave them to rest in a cool place for about 1 hour, then wash and dry the slices.

Beat the eggs in a bowl with a pinch of salt and pepper. Mix the Pecorino cheese with the breadcrumbs. Roll each slice of aubergine in the flour, then dip it in the beaten eggs and then in the mixture of breadcrumbs and Pecorino cheese, making sure that each coating covers the slice completely. Heat plenty of vegetable oil in a frying pan; place the slices of aubergine in the pan a few at a time and brown. Remove them with a slotted spoon and, after draining, place them on a plate covered with a double sheet of kitchen paper to absorb the excess oil; continue to fry the others. Finally arrange the aubergine slices on a serving dish.

Vegetables in Puff Pastry

Sfogliata di Verdure

To serve 6

1 lb/450 g puff pastry

1 small onion

2 courgettes

1 large tomato

1 red pepper

1 egg

dried oregano

plain flour

olive oil

knob of butter

Preparation and cooking time: 1 hour plus any defrosting time

Pre-heat the oven to 375°F/190°C/gas mark 5.

1) Defrost the pastry if necessary and roll out thinly to ⅛ inch/3 mm thickness on a floured pastry board. Cut out two 5 × 12 inch/13 × 30 cm rectangles.

2) From one of the rectangles cut out a frame ¾ inch/2 cm wide, and discard the centre. Brush the edge of the other rectangle with beaten egg yolk.

3) Lay the frame over the rectangle to form a border and brush it with the egg yolk. Put it on a baking tray and cook in the oven for 20 minutes.

4) Wash and dry the pepper. You can remove the outer skin by holding it carefully over a gas flame (or it can be placed for a little while in the oven). Remove the seeds, peel and chop it. Clean, wash and dice tomato and courgette.

5) Finely chop the onion and fry it until brown in a pan with 3 tablespoons of olive oil. Add the courgette, cook for 10 minutes, then add the tomatoes and pepper.

6) Season with salt, papper, oregano and cook for 15 minutes. Transfer the cooked pastry to a serving dish and spoon in the cooked vegetable mixture.

Serve hot or warm.

1

2

3

4

5

6

Mushrooms à la Grecque

Funghi di Coltura Ateniesi

To serve 6

¾-1 lb/400 g small fresh mushrooms

5 tablespoons strained lemon juice

olive oil

1 bay leaf

2 garlic cloves

large bunch of parsley

1 small stick celery

4-5 black peppercorns

1 red onion

Preparation and cooking time: about 50 minutes plus cooling

Trim the stems of the mushrooms and peel or wipe the caps. Rinse them well. Place on the heat a saucepan with 1 pint/500 ml of water, the lemon juice, 5 tablespoons of olive oil, bay leaf, 2 halved garlic cloves, 3-4 chopped parsley sprigs, the chopped celery, 4-5 peppercorns and a good pinch of salt; bring to the boil, then simmer for a couple of minutes, half-covered.

Meanwhile quarter the mushrooms, then plunge them into the liquid and simmer for about 15 minutes. Chop a small handful of parsley and cut 6 thin rings from the onion. When the mushrooms are ready pour them into a bowl with the hot cooking liquid, removing the garlic and bay leaf. Leave to cool at room temperature, then sprinkle with the chopped parsley, garnish with the onion rings and serve. These mushrooms, kept in the liquid and covered with cling film, will keep for 3-4 days in the refrigerator.

Cheese 'Tear-drops'

Gocce Ovette

To serve 6

1 egg

6 slices fresh white bread

6 slices Pariser cheese

mayonnaise

1 sprig parsley

Preparation time: about 30 minutes

Hard-boil the egg and cool it under cold running water. Using a pastry-cutter, cut 12 tear-drop shapes out of the bread and cheese. Spread each piece of bread with a little mayonnaise and place the pieces of cheese on top, fitting the shapes carefully together.

Shell the egg and chop it coarsely, together with a sprig of parsley. Place a little of this mixture on each 'tear-drop', leaving a border of about ¼ inch/5 mm. Arrange on a tray or plate garnished with parsley and serve.

Mushrooms à la grecque

Artichoke and Swiss Cheese Pie

Sfogliata Vallese

To serve 6

8 oz/250 g puff pastry

a little butter

1 tablespoon breadcrumbs

6 oz/175 g rindless Appenzell cheese, thinly sliced

1 lb/500 g frozen or tinned artichoke hearts

2 oz/50 g grated Sbrinz cheese

3 large eggs

2-3 sprigs parsley

Preparation and cooking time: about 1 hour plus thawing

Defrost the puff pastry if necessary, roll it out and line a 9-inch/22 cm round buttered pie dish with it. Prick the base of the pastry with a fork, then sprinkle over a tablespoon of breadcrumbs and cover with the thin slices of Appenzell cheese. Pre-heat the oven to 375°F/190°C/gas mark 5.

Following the instructions on the packet, cook the artichoke hearts in boiling salted water, then drain and leave them to dry for a few minutes on a plate covered with a tea-towel. Liquidize the artichokes. Put the pulp in a bowl. Add the grated Sbrinz, the eggs, chopped parsley, a little salt and a grinding of pepper. Mix thoroughly, then pour the mixture into the pie dish over the cheese.

Bake for 35 minutes in the lower part of the oven until the pastry is cooked through. Remove the pie from the oven, leave it to rest for a few minutes and then serve.

Endive Pie

Teglia di Scarola

To serve 6

3 oz/75 g butter

9 half-slices square white bread

18 oz/500 g Batavian endive

1 medium onion

2 large garlic cloves

parsley

olive oil

½ stock cube

2 oz/50 g grated Parmesan cheese

2 oz/50 g grated Emmental cheese

1 large egg

⅓ pint/200 ml single cream

Preparation and cooking time: about 1¼ hours

Pre-heat the oven to 375°F/190°C/gas mark 5. Butter a rectangular 9 x 6 inch/22 × 15 cm pie dish. Cover the bottom with the slices of bread, making sure they fit perfectly. Parboil, dry and finely shred the endive and slice the onion. Chop the 2 large garlic cloves finely, removing the green centres. Wash, dry and finely chop a handful of parsley. Melt the remaining butter in a frying pan with the oil and sauté the onion, garlic and parsley. Then add the shredded endive and crumble in the stock cube. Fry gently for about 10 minutes, stirring from time to time with a wooden spoon.

Combine the Parmesan cheese with the Emmental cheese and spread half over the bread in the bottom of the dish. Then make an even layer of the endive mixture and sprinkle over the remaining cheese. Beat the egg with the cream, a little salt and grated nutmeg in a bowl, then pour the mixture over the rest. Bake for about 30 minutes until the surface is golden brown. Remove from the oven and set aside for a few minutes before serving.

Artichoke and Swiss cheese pie

Italic Cheese Tart

Crostata Italica

To serve 4

8 oz/250 g plain flour

6 oz/150 g butter

3 medium onions

a little butter and flour

1 tablespoon fresh breadcrumbs

8 oz/250 g Italic cheese

3 eggs

¼ pint/150 ml milk

Preparation and cooking time: about 1¼ hours

Sift the flour and a pinch of salt. Cut 4 oz/100 g of the butter into small pieces and rub it into the flour until the mixture resembles fine breadcrumbs. Mix in enough water to make a soft, but not too sticky, dough. Roll the dough into a ball, wrap it in greaseproof paper and place in the refrigerator for 30 minutes.

Meanwhile thinly slice the onions and fry them gently in 1 oz/25 g of butter. Season with a little salt and pepper. If necessary, add a little water to prevent browning. Pre-heat the oven to 350°F/180°C/gas mark 4.

Roll out the pastry on a floured board. Grease and flour an 11-inch/25 cm pie dish and line it with the pastry. Pierce the base with a fork and sprinkle over about a tablespoon of the fresh breadcrumbs.

Grate the Italic cheese. Beat the eggs and milk in a bowl, season with salt and pepper and add the onions and cheese. Pour the mixture on to the pastry and bake in the lower part of the oven for 35-40 minutes. Serve hot.

Omelette Cooked in the Oven

'Frittata' della Fornarina

To serve 4

1 small onion

olive oil

1 very large ripe tomato

1 bunch fresh basil

½ stock cube

4 eggs

1 oz/25 g grated Parmesan cheese

butter

Preparation and cooking time: about 50 minutes

Pre-heat the oven to 350°F/180°C/gas mark 4. Finely slice the onions and fry gently in 4 tablespoons of olive oil. Dice the tomato and add it to the onion with 2 basil leaves and half a crumbled stock cube. Increase the heat and let the tomato dry out thoroughly. Remove from the heat and leave to cool. Discard the basil.

Beat the eggs in a bowl and season with a little salt and pepper. Add the grated Parmesan cheese and the cold tomato mixture.

Butter a 10 inch/25 cm round ovenproof dish. Cut out a circle of foil or greaseproof paper the same size as the dish, butter it and place it in the bottom of the dish, making sure that it sticks well. Pour in the egg mixture and cook in the oven for about 20 minutes.

As soon as the top of the omelette is golden brown, remove the dish from the oven and turn it out on to a plate, discarding the foil or paper. Slice, garnish with fresh basil leaves and serve.

Omelette cooked in the oven

Eggs in Rich Sauce
Uova alla Ricca

To serve 4

white wine vinegar

8 eggs and 1 egg yolk

2 oz/50 g butter

flour

⅓ pint/200 ml milk

nutmeg

2 oz/50 g grated Emmental cheese

1 small black tinned truffle

tender celery leaves

Preparation and cooking time: about 40 minutes

Put a fairly wide, low-sided saucepan on to heat with plenty of water; when it comes to the boil, salt it and add 2 tablespoons of vinegar, then lower the heat so that the water just simmers. Break 8 eggs, one at a time, into a small plate or bowl, then slide them very carefully into the boiling water. With a spoon, try to collect the white above the yolks, then leave the eggs to poach uncovered for about 6 minutes.

Remove them one at a time with a slotted spoon and put them immediately into a bowl of lukewarm water. After a few minutes put them to dry on a plate covered with a double sheet of kitchen paper, and lay another sheet of paper gently on top. As soon as the eggs are dry, trim of any ragged fringes of egg white and arrange them on a buttered overproof serving dish. Pre-heat the oven to 425°F/220°C/gas mark 7.

Melt 1 oz/25 g of the butter in a small saucepan, add 1 oz/25 g of sieved flour and stir with a small whisk to prevent lumps forming. Pour the boiling milk in a thin stream on to this roux, then bring the sauce to the boil, stirring all the time. Salt moderately, add a little pepper and ground nutmeg, then remove from the heat, mix in the egg yolk and the grated Emmental cheese.

Pour the sauce over the eggs and place a thin slice of black truffle on each one. Pour over the remaining lukewarm melted butter and place in the oven for 2-3 minutes. Serve immediately,

Ligurian Pie
'Torta' Ligure

To serve 6-8

12 oz/350 g puff pastry

2 fresh artichokes

juice of ½ lemon

1 medium onion

1 garlic clove

a little parsley

about 3 oz/75 g butter

olive oil

⅕ pint/125 ml stock (or use stock cube)

6 oz/150 g parboiled, drained lettuce

½ mushroom-flavoured stock cube

flour

¼ pint/150 ml milk

2 eggs

2 oz/50 g grated Parmesan cheese

1 tablespoon breadcrumbs

Preparation and cooking time: 1½ hours plus any thawing

Defrost the puff pastry if necessary. Trim the artichokes and peel the stems, placing them in cold water with the juice of half a lemon. Chop the onion and soften it, together with a garlic clove and a small bunch of parsley, in a knob of the butter and 2 tablespoons of oil. Drain the artichokes well, slice them thinly and add to the mixture in the pan. Brown for a few minutes, then pour over the stock and cook in a covered pan until the artichokes are tender and have absorbed all the liquid. Pre-heat the oven to 400°F/200°C/gas mark 6.

Chop the lettuce and sauté it in 1 oz/ 25 g of butter; sprinkle with the mushroom-flavoured cube and the flour. Stir, and gradually pour in the boiling milk. Leave to simmer for a few minutes, then stir and pour into a bowl. Stir the artichokes, then add them to the lettuce mixture, mixing well. Add the beaten eggs, the Parmesan cheese and a little salt.

Line a buttered oval pie dish measuring about 12 x 8 inches/30 × 20 cm with the puff pastry, prick the base and sprinkle with about 1 tablespoon of breadcrumbs. Pour in the prepared mixture and cook in the oven for about 30 minutes.

Ligurian pie

Cheese and Walnut Pie

Torta di Formaggio e Noci

To serve 4

12 oz/300 g puff pastry

a little flour

a little butter

4oz/100 g Emmental cheese

3 oz/75 g walnuts

2 eggs plus 1 egg white

1 tablespoon Calvados liqueur

ground nutmeg

Preparation and cooking time: about 50 minutes plus any defrosting time

Defrost the pastry, if necessary, and roll out on a floured surface to a thickness of ⅛ inch/3-4 mm. Butter a 9 inch/22 cm ovenproof pie dish and line it with the pastry.

Cut the Emmental cheese into small pieces and liquidize with the walnuts. Place in a bowl and stir in 2 eggs, the Calvados, a pinch of salt and pepper and a little ground nutmeg. Pour this mixture into the pie shell.

Pre-heat the oven to 375°F/190°C/gas mark 5. Roll out the remaining pastry and cover the pie with it. Brush the edges with the lightly beaten egg white and seal the lid to the sides of the pastry. Bake in the lower part of the oven for about 30 minutes or until golden brown. Serve hot.

Valdostana Fondue

'Fondua' Valdostana

To serve 3

12 oz/300 g Fontina cheese

¼ pint/150 ml tepid milk

1 oz/25 g butter

3 egg yolks

3 slices white bread

Preparation and cooking time: about 20 minutes plus 2 hours' soaking

Cut the rind off the cheese, slice it into a bowl and cover it with the milk. Leave it to soak for a couple of hours, stirring.

Melt the butter in a fondue pan, add the cheese and place over a simmering *bain-marie*. Stir continuously until the cheese melts, then raise the heat and stir more briskly, adding the egg yolks one by one, making sure each is perfectly incorporated before adding the next. Continue stirring until the cheese is completely melted and dissolved. Pour the fondue into warmed individual dishes and serve with toasted bread.

Broccoli with Scrambled Eggs

Broccoletti con le Uova Strapazzate

To serve 4

2 lb/1 kg green broccoli

olive oil

1 garlic clove

1 small piece red chilli pepper

2 large eggs

2 tablespoons grated Pecorino cheese

pepper

Preparation and cooking time: about 1 hour

Trim the broccoli and cut it into pieces, including the tender stalks of the larger pieces. Break the larger heads into florets. Put into lightly salted cold water for 30 minutes, then rinse well. Boil a large saucepanful of water and add salt. Put in the broccoli and cook for 5 minutes. When the broccoli is tender, remove with a slotted spoon, drain carefully and place on a large sloping dish for a few minutes.

In the meantime, heat 4 tablespoons of olive oil in a frying pan with the lightly crushed garlic and the chilli. Discard the garlic and chilli and replace with the broccoli. Shake the pan to ensure it does not stick to the bottom. Beat the eggs and the Pecorino cheese in a bowl and season with a little salt and pepper. Heat 3 tablespoons of olive oil in a small frying pan and, when it is hot, pour in the eggs. Continue stirring with a fork until they take on a creamy consistency. Arrange the broccoli on a hot serving dish and top with the scrambled eggs. Serve immediately.

*Cheese and walnut pie (left); **broccoli with scrambled eggs** (right)*

Rice with Tomatoes and Mushrooms

Riso al Pomodoro con Funghi

To serve 4

12 oz/350 g mushrooms (preferably ceps)

butter

olive oil

1 garlic clove

2-3 sprigs fresh parsley

12 oz/350 g rice

⅓ pint/200 ml tomato sauce

grated Parmesan cheese

Preparation and cooking time: about 1 hour 10 minutes

Clean the mushrooms carefully, scraping any earth from the stalks and wiping the caps. Rinse quickly, dry carefully and then slice them. Melt 1 oz/25 g of butter with 3 tablespoons of olive oil and the crushed garlic clove. Add the mushrooms and cook for about 10 minutes, then add some pepper and the chopped parsley.

Meanwhile bring to the boil a pan of water, add salt and cook the rice in it until barely soft. Drain, turn on to a heated deep serving dish and coat with the boiling tomato sauce. Add the mushrooms, which should also be very hot.

Serve immediately with grated Parmesan cheese.

Pilau with Eggs and Creamed Asparagus

Pilaf con Uova e Crema d'Asparagi

To serve 5

1¼ pints/750 ml light stock (or use stock cube)

1 medium onion

4 oz/100 g butter

12 oz/350 g rice

8 oz/250 g boiled green asparagus tips

flour

⅓ pint/200 ml milk

½ stock cube

nutmeg

3 eggs

1 oz/25 g grated Parmesan cheese

3 tablespoons/50 ml single cream

olive oil

Preparation and cooking time: about 40 minutes

Put the stock on to heat slowly. Pre-heat the oven to 400°F/200°C/gas mark 6. Finely chop half the onion and soften it in a large knob of butter, melted in an ovenproof pan. Add the rice and let it brown lightly for a few moments, stirring with a wooden spoon. Then moisten it with the boiling stock, bring back to the boil, and put in the oven for 15 minutes or a little longer, until the rice has absorbed almost all the liquid.

Meanwhile soften the remaining onion, sliced very thinly, in 1 oz/25 g of butter, then add three-quarters of the asparagus tips, in small pieces, and let the flavours mingle for a few moments. Sprinkle in a heaped tablespoon of sifted flour, stir and immediately pour on the boiling milk in a thin stream. Stirring continuously, bring the sauce to the boil, flavouring it with the crumbled half stock cube, the pepper and nutmeg. Then, keeping it hot in a *bain-marie,* whisk it for a couple of minutes.

Beat the eggs with the grated

Parmesan cheese, the cream and a little salt and pepper. In a large frying pan melt a large knob of butter with 2 tablespoons of olive oil. When the butter and oil are hot, pour in the beaten eggs and beat vigorously with a fork until they are very creamy.

Take the rice out of the oven, quickly stir in the remaining, softened butter, cut in pieces, and arrange the rice in individual serving dishes. Pour over the beaten eggs, then the boiled asparagus cream, and arrange the reserved asparagus tips on top. Serve immediately.

Polenta and Cheese Pudding

'Budino' di Polenta al Formaggio

To serve 6-8

¾ pint/450 ml milk

1½ stock cubes

12 oz/350 g quick-cooking polenta

2 oz/50 g butter

olive oil

4 oz/100 g grated Parmesan cheese

1 oz/25 g plain flour

2 egg yolks

Polenta and cheese pudding

4 oz/100 g Fontina cheese

celery leaves

Preparation and cooking time: about 40 minutes

Heat 2 pints/1.5 litres of water and ¼ pint/150 ml of milk. Add a little salt and crumble in a stock cube. As soon as the mixture begins to boil, sprinkle in the polenta, stirring first with a whisk and then a wooden spoon. Cook for about 20 minutes, then remove from the heat. Mix in 1 oz/25 g of butter in small knobs and half the Parmesan cheese, stirring constantly. Put the polenta into a greased mould with fluted sides. Cover with a cloth and prepare the sauce.

Melt the remaining butter in a saucepan and incorporate the flour, mixing with a small whisk. Boil the remaining milk and combine it with the roux a little at a time. Stirring constantly, bring the sauce to the boil and flavour with half a stock cube. Remove from the heat and add the 2 egg yolks, the remaining Parmesan cheese and the Fontina cheese cut into small pieces. Mix well, then pour the boiling sauce over the polenta which has been turned out on to a deep dish. For garnish, place the chopped celery leaves in the centre of the polenta pudding and serve immediately. This substantial hot starter can also be served as a main course.

Artichoke Pilau

Pilaf ai Carciofi

To serve 4

4 small artichokes

juice of ½ lemon

olive oil

2 tablespoons dry white wine

1½ pint/1 litre stock (or use stock cube)

3 sprigs fresh parsley

¼ stock cube

1 small garlic clove

ground thyme

1 small onion

2 oz/50 g butter

12 oz/350 g rice

1 oz/25 g grated Parmesan cheese

Preparation and cooking time: about 50 minutes

Trim the artichokes, remove the tough outer leaves and put them in a bowl of water with the lemon juice. When they are all prepared, drain them and place them stalks upwards in a pan that will just hold them. Pour 3 tablespoons of oil, the white wine and 6 tablespoons of the cold stock over them. Add the parsley, the crumbled quarter stock cube, the chopped garlic and a pinch of thyme. Cover and cook over a low heat, without lifting the lid, for about 30 minutes or until tender.

Meanwhile, heat the remaining stock. Pre-heat the oven to 400°F/200°C/gas mark 6. Chop the onion finely and sauté it in 1 oz/25 g of butter in a flameproof dish. Add the rice, stir with a wooden spoon and let it brown for a few moments, then pour in the boiling stock and stir again. Return it to the boil. Cover with a sheet of buttered foil and put it in the oven for about 15 minutes, until the rice has absorbed all the liquid and is dry and fluffy. Take it out of the oven and fork in the remaining butter and the grated cheese. Turn it into a heated serving dish, place the quartered artichokes on top, garnish with fresh parsley and serve.

Artichoke and Quartirolo Cheese Pie

Teglia di Carciofi e Quartirolo

To serve 8

1 lb/500 g puff pastry

4 artichokes

juice of ½ lemon

1 small onion

1 large garlic clove

a handful of parsley

olive oil

2 oz/50 g butter

6 tablespoons/100 ml white wine

¼ pint/150 ml stock (or use stock cube)

a pinch of thyme

1 oz/25 g flour

¼ pint/150 ml milk

2 oz/50 g grated Parmesan cheese

2 eggs

8 oz/250 g Quartirolo cheese

1 tablespoon breadcrumbs

Preparation and cooking time: about 1½ hours plus any defrosting time

Defrost the pastry if using frozen. Clean the artichokes, stalks as well, and as they are ready put them in a bowl of cold water with the juice of half a lemon. Finely chop the onion with the garlic and parsley and fry in the olive oil and half the butter.

Drain the artichokes well, cut them in half and remove the chokes. Slice them thinly and add them to the frying pan. Stir with a wooden spoon. Slice the stalks horizontally and add those too. After a few minutes pour in the wine and allow it to evaporate almost entirely. Bring the stock to the boil and pour it in. Stir well and turn the heat down to the minimum. Season with a pinch of thyme and cover the pan. Cook the artichokes until nearly all the liquid has been absorbed, then

sprinkle with the sieved flour. Mix and pour in the boiling milk, stirring constantly. Simmer for a few minutes and add salt to taste. Pre-heat the oven to 350°F/180°C/gas mark 4.

Purée the artichoke mixture. Mix the Parmesan cheese and 2 eggs into the purée, stirring vigorously. Cut the Quartirolo cheese into thin slices. Roll out the pastry to a thickness of ⅛ inch/3 mm, then line a buttered 14 x 8 inch/34 x 20 cm pie dish with low sides. Prick the pastry with a fork and sprinkle with a fine layer of breadcrumbs. Arrange the slices of Quartirolo cheese in the dish and then pour over the artichoke purée. Trim the pastry around the edges of the dish and roll out to make a cover for the pie, making sure it sticks to the pastry beneath. Prick the surface with a fork and bake in the lower part of the oven for about 35 minutes until it is cooked and golden brown. Serve piping hot.

Artichoke and quartirolo cheese pie *(centre right)*

DESSERTS

Italian desserts can range from a seasonal fruit salad to a delicious cake or pastry, or a festive *panettone*. Well-known sweets like *zabaglione* and profiteroles, which are found in most Italian restaurants, can easily be made at home, with delicious results; and real Italian ice cream, made from fresh fruit juices, eggs, sugar and cream, is not only simple to make but tastes far superior to any manufactured ice cream.

Bananas with Pistachios

Banane 'Rosate' al Pistacchio

To serve 4

4 ripe bananas

1 oz/25 g sugar

4 tablespoons rum

1 oz/25 g pistachio nuts

5 tablespoons red fruit or rose hip jam

4-5 rose petals

Preparation time: about 20 minutes

Peel the bananas and halve them lengthwise. Lay them out on a large dish and sprinkle with the sugar and rum. Leave to stand in a cool place.

Meanwhile, parboil the pistachios in salted water for a couple of minutes. Peel them while they are still hot and chop them finely. Place the jam in a bowl and stir until smooth. Place it in the centre of a serving dish and arrange the bananas around it. Pour the rum marinade over the bananas and top with the pistachios. Garnish with 4-5 rose petals (if available) and serve immediately.

Netted Plums

Prugne nella Rete

To serve 4

For the sponge cake:

a little flour

2 oz/50 g butter

3 eggs plus 1 yolk

8 oz/250 g sugar

grated rind of 1 lemon

a little vanilla sugar

4 oz/100 g plain flour

2 oz/50 g cornflour

For the topping:

10 large yellow plums

1 oz/25 g sugar

6 tablespoons/100 ml dry white wine

7 oz/200 g plum jam

⅓ pint/200 ml Amaretto liqueur

For the caramel:

4 oz/100 g sugar

Preparation and cooking time: about 2 hours

To make the sponge: pre-heat the oven to 350°F/180°C/gas mark 4. Grease and flour a 9 inch/23 cm dome-shaped cake pan. Melt 1 oz/25 g of butter and leave it to cool while beating together 3 whole eggs and 1 yolk with the sugar, if possible using an electric whisk to make the mixture light and frothy. Stir in the grated lemon rind, the vanilla sugar, cornflour and most of the sifted flour. Lastly, add the cool melted butter. Turn the mixture into a cake tin and bake it in the oven for 35 minutes. It is done when a skewer comes out clean. Turn the sponge out to cool on a wire rack.

While the sponge is cooking, wash and dry the plums, cut them in half, remove the stones and place them in a pan in a single layer. Sprinkle them with 1 oz/25 g of sugar, add white wine and cook them over a moderate heat with the lid on for 5 minutes. Take them out of the pan and drain them on kitchen paper.

Add the plum jam and half the liqueur to the juice left in the pan. Stir over a low heat until it becomes a thick syrup. When the sponge is cool, cut it into 3 layers, moisten them with the remaining liqueur, spread them with the jam mixture (reserving 2 tablespoons) and reassemble the gateau on a serving plate. Spread the remaining jam on top and cover it with the cooked plum halves. Leave it in a cool place (not the refrigerator) while you prepare the caramel.

To make the caramel: place the sugar with 3 tablespoons of water over a low heat, stirring gently at first until the sugar is completely dissolved. Cook until the sugar has completely caramelized. Dip a wooden spoon into the caramel and run it crisscross fashion over all the plums, like an irregular net. Serve immediately.

Amaretto Ice Cream
Gelato all'Amaretto

To serve 6

1 pint/500 ml milk

1 vanilla pod

5 egg yolks

6 oz/150 g sugar

4 oz/100 g small macaroons

4 tablespoons Amaretto liqueur

Preparation and cooking time: 30 minutes plus freezing time
Pour the milk into a saucepan; add the vanilla pod and slowly bring to the boil, then strain, discarding the pod, and leave to cool.

Meanwhile beat the 5 egg yolks with a pinch of salt and the sugar until soft and frothy. Stir in the lukewarm milk, pouring it in a trickle, and whisk until well blended. Then pour the mixture back into the saucepan, place on a very low heat and, stirring constantly, heat until it is about to boil.

Remove from the heat and strain the liquid through a fine sieve, then leave to cool at room temperature, stirring occasionally. Add the finely crumbled macaroons and Amaretto liqueur. Place in the refrigerator for about 1 hour, then pour the mixture into an ice cream machine or container and let it freeze.

Torrone Ice Cream
Gelato al Torroncino

To serve 6

6 oz/150 g assorted crystallized fruit

4 tablespoons Maraschino liqueur

4 oz/100 g *torrone* (Italian nougat)

1 pint/500 ml fresh milk

1 vanilla pod

7 oz/200 g sugar

4 egg yolks

Preparation and cooking time: 30 minutes plus freezing time
Coarsely chop the crystallized fruit, of different colours and flavours, place it in a small bowl and moisten it with the Maraschino. Pound the *torrone* to a powder. In a saucepan heat most of the milk with the vanilla pod and the sugar. When the milk is hot and the sugar has dissolved, discard the vanilla pod.

Beat the 4 egg yolks in a bowl adding first the cold milk then the hot, pouring in a trickle and stirring constantly. When the ingredients are well mixed, pour back into the saucepan and heat for a couple of minutes, stirring, without bringing it to boil. Remove the saucepan from the heat and strain the mixture into a bowl. Let it cool, stirring occasionally, then leave it for at least 1 hour in the refrigerator. Just before placing it in an ice cream machine or container mix in the crystallized fruit and the *torrone*.

Hazelnut Ice Cream
Gelato alla Nocciola

To serve 6

4 oz/100 g shelled hazelnuts

1 pint/500 ml milk

1 vanilla pod

6 oz/150 g sugar

5 egg yolks

Preparation and cooking time: 45 minutes plus freezing time
Spread the hazelnuts over the base of a baking tray and roast at 350°F/180°C/gas mark 4 for 7-8 minutes. Remove from the oven and, while still hot, place them in a metal sieve and rub them with the palm of your hand to remove their outer skins. Let them cool completely, then pound to a powder in a mortar or blender.

Heat most of the milk in a saucepan with the vanilla pod, a pinch of salt and the sugar. Beat the 5 egg yolks with a small whisk, adding first the cold milk then the hot little by little and stirring constantly.

When the ingredients are well blended, pour the mixture back into the saucepan and place it on the heat for 2 minutes, stirring constantly and without letting the mixture boil. Immediately remove it from the heat and strain the liquid into a bowl. Leave to cool, stirring occasionally, then add the ground hazelnuts. Finally pour the mixture into an ice cream machine or container and freeze it.

Chocolate Ice Cream
Gelato al Cioccolato

To serve 6

1 pint/500 ml milk

1 vanilla pod

5 egg yolks

6 oz/150 g sugar

1 tablespoon cocoa powder

4 oz/100 g plain cooking chocolate

1 egg white

Preparation and cooking time: 30 minutes plus freezing time
Pour most of the milk into a saucepan, add the vanilla pod and slowly bring it almost to the boil; remove from the heat and let it cool, then strain through a fine sieve, discarding the vanilla pod.

Beat the 5 egg yolks in a bowl with the sugar and the sieved cocoa until soft and smooth. Add first the cold milk, then the hot, pouring it in a trickle and whisking constantly. Pour the mixture back into the saucepan and place it over a low heat until it is about to boil, stirring constantly.

Remove it from the heat and add the grated chocolate, stirring well until it has melted and blended in. Strain the mixture through a fine sieve and let it cool completely before pouring it into an ice cream machine or container. Halfway through the freezing process, add one egg white, whisked to a froth, to make the ice cream smoother and softer.

Vanilla Ice Cream

Gelato alla Vaniglia

To serve 6

1 pint/500 ml milk

6 oz/150 g sugar

1 small vanilla pod

5 egg yolks

1 egg white

Preparation and cooking time: 30 minutes plus freezing time
Heat most of the milk in a saucepan with the sugar, a pinch of salt and the vanilla pod until about to boil.

Meanwhile beat the 5 egg yolks then add, little by little, first the cold milk, then the hot, stirring constantly. When the ingredients are well blended, pour the mixture back into the saucepan and heat for about 2 minutes, stirring.

Pour the mixture into a bowl and let it cool, stirring occasionally. Pour it into an ice cream machine or container, straining it through a fine sieve. Halfway through the process add 1 egg white whisked to a froth with a pinch of salt so that the ice cream will be very smooth and soft.

Rum and Coffee Ice Cream

Gelato di Caffè al Rum

To serve 6

1 pint/500 ml fresh milk

rind of ½ lemon

5 egg yolks

6 oz/150 g sugar

6 tablespoons/100 ml strong black coffee

2 tablespoons dark rum

Preparation and cooking time: 20 minutes plus freezing time
Bring the milk to the boil in a saucepan with the lemon rind, then let it cool. Beat the 5 egg yolks to a froth with the sugar, then add the warm milk, pouring it in a trickle through a sieve. Discard the lemon rind. Blend all the

ingredients thoroughly with a small whisk, then pour the mixture back into the saucepan. Add a pinch of salt and place the saucepan on a very low heat, stirring constantly, until the mixture is about to boil.

Remove the saucepan from the heat and strain the liquid through a fine sieve, then stir in the strong coffee and 2 tablespoons of rum. Leave the mixture to cool, first at room temperature, and then for at least 1 hour in the refrigerator. Then pour the mixture into an ice cream machine or container and freeze.

Pistachio Ice Cream

Gelato al Pistacchio

To serve 6

4 oz/100 g pistachio nuts

8 oz/250 g sugar

1 pint/500 ml milk

1 vanilla pod

5 egg yolks

Preparation and cooking time: 30 minutes plus freezing time
Plunge the pistachio nuts into salted boiling water for 1 minute, and shell them. Pound them in a mortar, adding a tablespoon of sugar from time to time, until they are reduced to powder.

Heat most of the milk with the remaining sugar and the vanilla pod and bring slowly to the boil, stirring occasionally with a wooden spoon. Remove from the heat and discard the vanilla pod. Place the 5 egg yolks in a bowl together with the powdered pistachio nuts. Beat with a small whisk to obtain a smooth mixture. Add first the cold milk, then the hot, poured in a trickle through a fine sieve, and stirring constantly.

When the ingredients are well blended, pour the mixture back into the saucepan, place it on the heat and stir until it is about to boil. At this point remove the saucepan from the heat, pour the mixture into a bowl and leave to cool, stirring occasionally. When cold pour into an ice cream machine or container and freeze.

Peach and Macaroon Pie

Crostata di Pesche all'Amaretto

To serve 6-8

a little butter and flour

4 oz/100 g plain flour

2 oz/50 g sugar

grated rind of ½ lemon

1 egg yolk

2 oz/50 g butter

1 tablespoon dry vermouth

12 small macaroons

6 tablespoons peach jam

1 tablespoon apricot brandy

2 large yellow peaches

1 tablespoon Amaretto liqueur

redcurrants

Preparation and cooking time: about 1 hour plus cooling
Pre-heat the oven to 375°F/190°C/gas mark 5. Butter and flour a round, smooth 10 inch/23 cm pie dish. Sift the flour and add a pinch of salt, the sugar and the grated lemon rind. Make a well in the centre and add the egg yolk, the softened butter, cut in small pieces, and the vermouth. Knead rapidly into a smooth dough, then roll out and line the prepared dish with it; prick the bottom of the pastry with a fork. Crumble over 7 macaroons. Set aside 2 tablespoons of peach jam, place the rest in a bowl and stir in the apricot brandy. Spread the jam evenly over the crumbs.

Peel, halve and stone the peaches, then cut them into equal slices and arrange them in a circle, slightly overlapping, on the pastry; in the centre put the remaining macaroons and sprinkle them with the Amaretto liqueur. Bake for about 40 minutes.

Remove the pie from the oven and let it cool in the dish; then place it on a large round plate. Melt the remaining jam over a low heat, strain it through a fine sieve and brush the peach slices and the macaroons with it. As soon as the glaze has cooled and is firm, garnish the pie with sprigs of redcurrants and serve.

Peaches with Pine-nuts

Pesche ai Pinoli

To serve 4

4 equal-sized yellow peaches, perfectly ripe

butter

1 clove

2 inch/5 cm piece lemon rind

2 tablespoons granulated sugar

6 tablespoons brandy

8 tablespoons pine-nuts

Preparation and cooking time: about 45 minutes
Remove the stems from the peaches, then wash and dry them; cut them in half with a small sharp knife and remove the stones. Melt a large knob of butter in a large saucepan, then arrange the 8 half-peaches on the bottom of the pan, cut side down. Fry very gently for a few moments with the pan uncovered, then add a clove and the piece of lemon rind. Sprinkle the fruit with 2 tablespoons of sugar and moisten with 6 tablespoons of brandy. Move the pan slightly to make sure the peaches aren't stuck to the bottom, then lower the heat to the minimum, cover, and cook the half-peaches for about 20 minutes.

Place the half-peaches, with the cut side upwards on a serving dish and in the hollow of each place a teaspoon of pine-nuts. Reduce the cooking liquid slightly, then strain it through a fine sieve directly on to the fruit. Serve immediately while still hot though peaches prepared in this way are also excellent lukewarm.

Almond Puffs

Sgonfietti alle Mandorle

To serve 8

6 oz/150 g almonds, shelled but not peeled

6 oz/150 g caster sugar

2 oz/50 g cornflour

6 egg whites

a little butter

Preparation and cooking time: about 40 minutes
Pre-heat the oven to 350°F/180°C/gas mark 4. Blanch the almonds in boiling water then peel them. Toast them lightly in the oven for a few minutes then leave them to cool. Turn the oven down to 300°F/150°C/gas mark 2. Coarsely grind 5 oz/125 g of the almonds and cut the rest into slivers. Pour the sugar into a bowl together with the ground almonds and sift in the cornflour. Whisk the egg whites until they are stiff and fold into the other ingredients using a gentle up-and-down movement so as not to deflate the egg whites.

Liberally butter 2 baking trays, then spoon dollops of the mixture a little larger than the size of a walnut on both trays and decorate with the almond slivers. Bake for about 20 minutes, until the meringues are slightly brown and firm to the touch. Remove them even if they are still a little sticky as they will harden on cooling. Lift the puffs off the trays with a metal spatula and cool them thoroughly before arranging them on a serving dish. They are best eaten as soon as they are cold.

Fruit Cup

Coppa di Frutta

To serve 4

½ pomegranate

2 tablespoons Cointreau

20 green grapes

1 oz/25 g sugar

juice of ½ lemon

4 ripe oranges

Preparation time: about 40 minutes
Peel the pomegranate and place the segments in a bowl. Sprinkle with the Cointreau and stir gently. Cover the bowl and place in a cool place. Allow the fruit to soak for about 15 minutes.

Wash and dry the grapes and cut each one lengthwise into 4 segments, taking care to remove the pips. Place the segments in a bowl and dust with 2 heaped tablespoons of sugar. Sprinkle with the juice of half a lemon, stir and put aside in a cool place for a few minutes.

Peel the oranges, taking care to remove all the pith. Divide the oranges into segments and place in a bowl, squeezing any juice remaining in the peel over them. Add the pomegranate and grape segments, together with their juices, to the orange segments and stir well. Keep in the refrigerator until ready to serve.

Fresh Apricot Compote

Composta di Albicocche

To serve 6

1¼ lb/600 g firm ripe apricots

4 oz/100 g apricot jam

1 tablespoon white rum

1 tablespoon apricot liqueur

grated rind of 1 lemon

1 lime for garnish

7 Maraschino cherries

Preparation time: about 15 minutes plus 1½ hours' soaking
Remove the stalks from the apricots and wipe them with a damp cloth. Halve them, remove the stones, and slice them into a basin. Strain the jam, dilute it with the rum and liqueur and add the grated lemon rind. Mix well and pour over the apricots, stirring carefully.

Cover the basin with cling film and leave in the least cold part of the refrigerator for at least 1½ hours giving it a gentle stir from time to time. Then distribute the apricots among 6 individual bowls. Garnish each one with 5 wafer-thin rings of lime and 5 slices of Maraschino cherry. Serve at once.

Peach and macaroon pie (above left) and peaches with pine-nuts; fruit cup (right)

Home-made Sultana Cake

Dolce Casereccio all'Uvetta

To make 2 cakes

about 6 oz/150 g butter

12 oz/350 g plain flour

4 oz/100 g sultanas

3 tablespoons/50 ml Strega liqueur

3 eggs

6 oz/150 g caster sugar

1 lemon with an unblemished rind

1 oz/25 g pine-nuts

1 teaspoon vanilla-flavoured baking powder

a little icing sugar

Preparation and cooking time: about 1¼ hours
Pre-heat the oven to 350°F/180°C/gas mark 4. The above ingredients will make 2 cakes, each to serve 5-6 people. Butter and flour a round fluted 1¼ pint/¾ litre mould and a rectangular 9 x 5 inch/22 x 12 cm one with about the same capacity. Soak the sultanas in the Strega liqueur. Whip the egg yolks, setting the whites aside, with the caster sugar, a pinch of salt and the grated lemon rind.

When you have a light frothy mixture, incorporate 4 oz/100 g cooled melted butter, mixing constantly and vigorously. Continue beating for a few minutes, then drain the sultanas and add these too, floured and mixed with the pine-nuts. Sift in 8 oz/250 g of flour mixed with the baking powder. Add 2 tablespoons of the Strega in which the sultanas were soaked.

Whip the egg whites with a pinch of salt until they are firm and carefully fold into the mixture which should be fairly stiff. Divide into 2 and pour into the moulds, shaking them lightly to eliminate air bubbles. Bake the rectangular cake for 30 minutes and the round one for 40 minutes. Remove from the oven and leave to cool.

Before serving sprinkle one or both cakes with powdered sugar. Serve with cream, or with zabaglione or custard. The cakes can be kept for 3-4 days in their moulds covered with foil. Leave in a cool place (not the refrigerator).

Little Doughnut Rings

Ciambelline 'Golose'

To serve 4-6

6 oz/150 g plain flour

grated rind of ½ lemon

2 oz/50 g sugar

butter

teaspoon baking powder

a little milk

cooking oil

Preparation and cooking time: 1½ hours
Mix the flour, a pinch of salt, the grated lemon rind, the sugar, butter and a teaspoon of baking powder into a soft, but not too sticky, dough with a little warm milk.

Divide the dough into little pieces and roll them in your hands to form thin cords ¼ inch/6 mm in diameter. Cut them into 5 inch/12 cm lengths. Join the ends of each cord to form rings. Place on a baking tray on a sheet of lightly oiled foil and leave to stand for 10 minutes.

Heat plenty of oil in a deep-frying pan and fry the rings, a few at a time, until golden brown. Make sure that the oil is hot but not boiling throughout cooking. Drain the rings on kitchen paper, arrange on a plate and serve.

Little doughnut rings

St Valentine's Heart
'Cuore' di San Valentino

To serve 6-8

8 oz/250 g puff pastry

8 macaroons

4 oz/100 g boiled, puréed chestnuts

2 oz/50 g icing sugar

2 tablespoons Amaretto liqueur

3 tablespoons very fresh Mascarpone cheese (or cream cheese)

½ oz/15 g cocoa powder

2 oz/50 g pine-nuts

2 oz/50 g sultanas

2 eggs

⅓ pint/200 ml whipping cream

10 pink sugar almonds

1 tablespoon coloured sugar crystals

a little flour

Preparation and cooking time: 1½ hours plus any thawing time
Defrost the puff pastry if necessary, then roll it out to about ⅛ inch/3 mm thick. Roll it round the rolling-pin, then unroll it on to a baking tray. Place on top of the pastry a mould or a piece of card cut into a heart shape that almost covers the pastry, and cut around it with a sharp knife. Discard the pastry trimmings. Prick the heart with a fork and leave to rest.

Pre-heat the oven to 375°F/190°C/ gas mark 5. Crumble 6 of the macaroons finely and put in a bowl with the puréed chestnuts, 1 oz/25 g sieved sugar, the Amaretto liqueur, the Mascarpone cheese and the cocoa powder. Stir well until smooth and creamy, then mix in the pine-nuts and 1 oz/20 g washed and dried sultanas. Bind the mixture with the 2 whole eggs, beating vigorously, then spread over the puff pastry to about ½ inch/ 1 cm from the edge. Bake on a low shelf for about 20 minutes.

Place the heart on a rack to cool. Meanwhile, crumble the rest of the macaroons very finely. Whip the cream

until it is quite firm, then put into a piping bag fitted with a round, fluted nozzle and pipe rosettes round the edge of the heart. Sieve the remaining icing sugar over the top, then decorate the cake with the rest of the sultanas, the remaining crumbled macaroons, the pink sugar almonds and the coloured sugar crystals. Serve immediately.

Chestnut Cup
Coppette di Castagne

To serve 4

1 lb/500 g chestnuts, boiled and peeled

4 oz/100 g caster sugar

4 tablespoons Cointreau

a little vanilla sugar

6 tablespoons/100 ml whipping cream

6 pistachio nuts

Preparation and cooking time: about 30 minutes plus cooling
Place the chestnuts in a bowl that just holds them. Heat the sugar with 3 tablespoons of water, letting it dissolve gradually then come to the boil. Take it off the heat, add the Cointreau and vanilla sugar, stir it and pour it over the chestnuts. Cover the bowl with cling film and leave it to cool completely, during which time the chestnuts will absorb much of the syrup.

Divide the chestnuts between 4 individual cups. Whip the cream until firm and, using a piping bag, decorate each cup with a ring of cream rosettes. Blanch the pistachio nuts for a few seconds in slightly salted boiling water, remove the skins and dry them on kitchen paper. Chop them finely and sprinkle them on the cream. Serve immediately, since the chestnuts are at their best straight after cooling.

St Valentine's heart

Little Love Biscuits

Biscottini d'Amore

To serve 6

8 oz/250 g plain flour

pinch of ground cinnamon

pinch of ground cloves

grated rind of ½ lemon

3 oz/75 g sugar

1 teaspoon baking powder

1 teaspoon vanilla essence

1 egg

4 oz/100 g butter

1 heaped teaspoon cocoa powder

1 teaspoon brandy

Preparation and cooking time: about 1 hour

Mix the flour with a pinch each of salt, cinnamon and cloves, the lemon rind and the sugar. Add the baking powder. Then make a well and add the whole egg, the vanilla essence and the softened butter cut into small pieces.

Knead all together quickly to give a smooth, even dough, then divide into 2 pieces, one twice as large as the other. Work 1 heaped teaspoon of sieved cocoa powder into the smaller piece of dough together with the brandy, kneading for a few minutes. Roll the larger piece out on the board sprinkled lightly with flour to a thickness of about ⅛ inch/3 mm. Then cut into shapes using a heart-shaped pastry cutter and arrange them on 1 or 2 buttered and floured baking trays. Knead together the remaining dough, roll out and cut out more shapes. Continue until all the dough is used up. Pre-heat the oven to 350°F/180°C/gas mark 4.

Now roll out the cocoa-flavoured dough and cut smaller heart shapes out of that, placing them centrally on top of the first hearts and pressing them down lightly to keep in place. Lastly place the small biscuits in the oven for about 12 minutes or until they are cooked and a light golden brown. Remove carefully from the tray using a palette knife and allow to cool on a rack. If desired, sprinkle with a little icing sugar before serving.

Chestnut 'Macaroons'

'Amaretti' di Castagne

To make 36 'macaroons'

8 oz/250 g chestnut purée

6 oz/150 g very fresh Mascarpone cheese

2 oz/50 g icing sugar

1 oz/25 g cocoa powder

¼ pint/150 ml brandy

3 dozen macaroons, plus 2 extra

Preparation time: about 30 minutes plus 1 hour's refrigeration

Combine the chestnut purée with the Mascarpone cheese in a bowl, then sift in the icing sugar and cocoa and mix to a smooth paste with half the brandy.

Put the mixture in a piping bag.

Pour the remaining brandy into a dish and soak the 3 dozen macaroons, flat side down, for a few seconds. As you remove them from the brandy, arrange them on a serving dish. Pipe out a large swirl of the chestnut purée on to each macaroon and place them in the refrigerator for at least an hour.

Crumble the 2 extra macaroons and sprinkle them over the others before serving.

Little love biscuits

Chestnut and Chocolate Roll

'Salame' di Castagne e Cioccolato

To serve 12

6 oz/150 g butter

4 oz/100 g icing sugar

3 oz/75 g cocoa powder

4 tablespoons Amaretto

6-7 macaroons

12 oz/350 g chestnuts, boiled and puréed

a little whipping cream

chocolate strands

Preparation and cooking time: about 40 minutes plus 3-4 hours' refrigeration Soften the butter and beat in a bowl with a wooden spoon until light and frothy. Sift in the icing sugar and the cocoa and mix in half the Amaretto. Grind the macaroons almost to a powder and add them, together with the chestnut paste and the remaining Amaretto, reserving 1 teaspoon. Blend all the ingredients together smoothly.

Pour the reserved teaspoon of Amaretto, diluted with 2 tablespoons of cold water, on to a sheet of foil. Spread the chestnut mixture on the foil and roll it up evenly and tightly. Seal the ends and refrigerate for 3-4 hours.

Just before serving, take it out of the refrigerator and remove the foil. Slice with a very sharp knife dipped in a bowl of hot water. Garnish, if you like, with a stripe of chocolate hundreds and thousands and serve with whipped cream.

Chestnut macaroons and **chestnut and chocolate roll** (top right)

Figs with Redcurrants and Ice Cream

Fichi Speziati con Ribes e Gelato

To serve 6

2 lb/1 kg fresh figs, not overripe

4 oz/100 g sugar

2 oz/50 g sultanas

ground cinnamon

ground ginger

a few whole cloves

6 tablespoons Alchermes

rind of 1 lemon

12 thin slices fruit loaf

pint of redcurrants

6 tablespoons vanilla ice cream

Preparation and cooking time: about 40 minutes plus 1 hour's marinating
Using a small, sharp knife, peel the figs. Cut each one into 4 or 6 according to size and place in a stainless steel saucepan. Add the sugar, sultanas, a large pinch of cinnamon, a pinch of ginger and a few cloves. Pour over 2 tablespoons of Alchermes liqueur. Cut a 3 inch/7 cm piece of lemon rind into needle-fine strips and add to the other ingredients. Cover and leave in a cool place for 1 hour.

Next, cook the figs over a low heat for about 15 minutes from the moment the liquid begins to simmer. Keep the pan uncovered and stir gently from time to time. Immerse the saucepan in cold water to cool.

Arrange the fruit loaf in a glass salad bowl and pour over 4 tablespoons of Alchermes. Spread the fig mixture on top and cover. Keep in the refrigerator until it is time to serve. Then sprinkle the stemmed, washed redcurrants on top and decorate with slivers of ice-cream.

Figs with redcurrants and ice cream
*(above) and **coronet cake***

Coronet Cake
Torta 'Coroncina'

To serve 8-10

a little butter

a little flour

3 eggs

6 oz/150 g caster sugar

2 sachets vanilla sugar

4 oz/100 g plain flour

2 oz/50 g potato flour

3 large, very ripe figs

⅓ pint/250 ml whipping cream

¼ pint/150 ml Cointreau liqueur

icing sugar

4 oz/100 g apricot jam

3 sprigs redcurrants

Preparation and cooking time: about 1¼ hours
Pre-heat the oven to 350°F/180°C/gas mark 4. Butter and flour a round 12 inch/30 cm cake ring (a Kugelhopf pan). Whisk the eggs with the sugar, the vanilla sugar and a pinch of salt until light and fluffy. Mix the flour and the potato flour and sift into the mixture. Fold in carefully using a wooden spoon with an up and down motion. Pour into the cake tin and bake for about 30 minutes until a wooden skewer plunged into the cake comes out clean. Turn out on to a rack and leave to cool.

Wipe the figs with a damp cloth, cut them in half and then into very thin slices using a small very sharp knife. Whip the cream until it is stiff. Cut the cake into 4 equal layers. Place the bottom round on a serving dish and pour over a third of the Cointreau. Then spread over a third of the whipped cream. Sprinkle with a teaspoon of icing sugar. Repeat the procedure with the other two layers and lightly press on the fourth.

Decorate the top with the fig slices to form a coronet. Heat the apricot jelly over a low heat and when it is runny, sieve through a fine strainer and brush the figs with it. Leave until the jelly has cooled. Complete the decoration with the redcurrants and serve at once.

Zabaglione Dessert
Chiaroscuro allo Zabaione

To serve 4-6

3 eggs

2 oz/50 g sugar

8 tablespoons dry Marsala wine

1 oz/25 g sultanas

⅓ pint/200 ml fresh whipping cream

12 chocolate-covered Savoy biscuits

Preparation and cooking time: about 30 minutes
Separate the eggs, placing the yolks in a saucepan and adding the sugar. Stir with a wooden spoon until pale and frothy, then stir in, one at a time, 6 tablespoons of the Marsala wine. Heat the mixture in a double boiler, beating constantly with a small whisk until it thickens. Leave to cool.

Meanwhile soak the sultanas for 15 minutes in warm water. When the zabaglione is cold, whip the cream and carefully stir in 3 tablespoons of it. Refrigerate the rest of the cream until it is required for decoration. Drain the sultanas thoroughly and stir in these too. Then spoon the mixture into a deepish square dish, distributing it evenly.

Pour 2 tablespoons of the Marsala into a soup bowl and add 2 tablespoons of water. Briefly dip the Savoy biscuits in the mixture, keeping the chocolate-coated side uppermost as you dip. Arrange the biscuits diagonally on top of the zabaglione cream as you proceed, alternating the chocolate sides with the plain. Cut the biscuits to fit the dish without leaving any gaps.

Put the remaining whipped cream into a piping bag with a fluted round nozzle and make a decorative border of swirls around the Savoy biscuits. Refrigerate until serving time.

Zabaglione dessert

Home-made Apple Cake

Torta di Mele, Casereccia

To serve 8

2 eggs

6 oz/150 g caster sugar

grated rind of 1 lemon

ground cinammon

ground cloves

6 oz/150 g flour

1 oz/25 g cornflour

5 tablespoons/80 ml milk

1 teaspoon baking powder

butter

breadcrumbs

1 lb/500 g apples, just ripe

3 oz/75 g apricot jam

Preparation and cooking time: about 1½ hours plus cooling

Pre-heat the oven to 350°F/180°C/gas mark 4. Beat the eggs with 4 oz/100 g of the sugar, a pinch of salt and the grated lemon rind. Then add another pinch of salt, followed by a pinch of cinnamon and a pinch of cloves. Combine the flour and the cornflour and sift these into the mixture. Gradually pour in the milk and sift in the baking powder. Mix all these ingredients together to form a smooth mixture.

Butter a 10 inch/25 cm cake tin and sprinkle it with breadcrumbs. Pour in the mixture. Peel and halve the apples, core and slice them, not too thinly. Arrange the slices on top of the mixture. Sprinkle with the rest of the sugar and intersperse with slivers of butter. Bake for about 45 minutes or until a toothpick comes out clean. Remove the cake from the oven and leave to cool. Heat the apricot jam over a low heat and, when it has melted, brush the surface of the cake with it and leave to cool. This home-made cake is best eaten the same day.

Coffee Cream Puff

Sfogliata alla Crema di Caffe

To serve 10

1 lb/500 g puff pastry

4 oz/100 g butter

8 almonds

1 egg

4 oz/100 g fresh Mascarpone cheese

4 oz/100 g icing sugar

2 tablespoons freeze-dried instant coffee

2 tablespoons coffee liqueur

2 tablespoons brandy

12 Savoy biscuits

¼ pint/150 ml Amaretto liqueur

Preparation and cooking time: about 1 hour plus any thawing

Defrost the pastry if necessary. Pre-heat the oven to 375°F/190°C/gas mark 5. Cut the butter into small pieces and leave to soften. Meanwhile, finely chop the almonds. Divide the pastry in half and roll out two rounds 10 inches/25 cm in diameter. Place on two baking trays and prick with a fork all over. Separate the egg yolk from the white and brush the surface of the pastry with the white. Bake for about 20 minutes, or until the pastry is golden brown. Remove from the oven and place on a cooling rack.

Meanwhile, beat the butter with the Mascarpone cheese and 4 oz/100 g icing sugar, ideally with an electric mixer. Incorporate the egg yolk, the instant coffee, the coffee liqueur and the brandy. The cream should be light and fluffy by the time you have finished. Lay one pastry round on top of the other and trim until they are exactly the same size. (Keep the offcuts.) Place one round on a round cardboard cake base and spread a third of the coffee cream over it. Soak the Savoy biscuits in the Amaretto and arrange these on top of the cream, breaking them up so that they do not jut out. Spread half the remaining cream over the biscuits. Then sprinkle over the crumbled pastry offcuts and press down the second

pastry round to ensure it adheres to the cream.

Cover the cake with the remaining cream and decorate with the chopped almonds. Place on a cake stand and refrigerate for at least 30 minutes before serving. Finally, sprinkle with a little icing sugar or decorate as you please.

Imperial Cake

Torta Imperiale

To serve 12

2 oz/50 g butter

about 8 oz/250 g plain flour

7 eggs plus 1 egg yolk

a little butter and flour

about 8 oz/250 g caster sugar

grated rind of ½ lemon

2 oz/50 g potato flour

3 oz/75 g almond biscuits

1 envelope vanilla sugar

generous ½ pint/350 ml milk

2 tablespoons Amaretto

¾ pint/400 ml whipping cream

2 oz/50 g icing sugar

9 tablespoons Cointreau

Preparation and cooking time: about 2 hours

Pre-heat the oven to 375°F/190°C/gas mark 5. Put ⅕ pint/125 ml of water in a small pan on the heat and add the butter and a pinch of salt. When the water comes to the boil and the butter melts, remove the pan from the heat for a moment and pour into it 3 oz/75 g of sieved flour, all at once, stirring vigorously with a wooden spoon. Put the pan back on the heat and continue cooking, still stirring, until the mixture begins to sizzle at the base. Then turn it out on to a plate, spread it out and leave to cool. Then put back into the pan and add 2 whole eggs, one at a time, beating vigorously and adding the second only when the first is completely mixed in. Put the mixture in a piping bag fitted with a smooth, round nozzle and pipe 35 equal amounts on to a buttered, floured baking tray, keeping the buns well spaced.

Place the tray in the oven for about 15 minutes or until the buns are well risen and golden brown. Allow to cool on a rack. Turn the oven down to 350°F/180°C/gas mark 4. Butter and flour a round cake tin 10 inches/25 cm in diameter with a smooth base and sides. Beat together 3 whole eggs with 6 oz/150 g of caster sugar, the grated rind of half a lemon and a small pinch of salt. When the mixture is smooth and fluffy, mix 4 oz/600 g of flour with the potato flour and sieve this into the mixture, folding in gently with a wooden spoon. Pour the mixture into the cake tin and place in the pre-heated oven for about 30 minutes, until a skewer or toothpick comes out clean. Turn out on to a tray and allow to cool.

Crush the biscuits, using a pestle and mortar (or break into small pieces and pulverize in a liquidiser). In a small pan, beat together 2 whole eggs, 1 egg yolk, 4 oz/100 g of caster sugar, 1 oz/25 g of sieved flour, a pinch of salt and the vanilla sugar. Gradually add the cold milk, mixing with a small whisk. Stirring continuously, bring to the boil, then remove from the heat and stand the pan in cold water to cool. Add the crushed biscuits and flavour with the Amaretto.

Whip the cream until very firm, add the sieved icing sugar, then put in a piping bag, fitted with a small, round, smooth nozzle. Fill the buns with some of this and keep the rest for decoration. Cut the cake into three layers, pour 3 tablespoons of Cointreau over each, spread with the cream and biscuit mixture, then put the layers back together. Arrange the filled buns on the top, then fill the space between them with the rest of the whipped cream. Keep the cake in a refrigerator (for 3-4 hours maximum) until ready to serve.

Plum Crescents
Mezzelune alla Marmellata

To serve 6-8

12 oz/350 g plain flour

¼ teaspoon baking powder

4 oz/100 g sugar

½ sachet vanilla sugar

grated rind of ½ lemon

2 eggs

3 oz/75 g butter

2 tablespoons anise liqueur

a little flour

1 jar plum jam

a little butter

a little icing sugar

Preparation and cooking time: about 1½ hours

Sift the flour and baking powder together. Add the sugar, the vanilla sugar and the grated lemon rind. Stir and then make a well in the centre. Place the eggs, the butter (cut into little pieces) and the anise liqueur in the well. Combine with the flour to form a firm, smooth dough. Pre-heat the oven to 350°F/180°C/gas mark 4.

Dust the board with a little flour and roll out the pastry to a thickness of ¼ inch/6 mm. Cut into 3 inch/7 cm circles with a serrated pastry cutter. Place a teaspoon of plum jam on each piece of pastry and fold each circle in half, sealing the edges.

Place the crescents on a buttered baking tray which has been sprinkled with a little flour. Make sure that they are not too close together as they will spread during cooking.

Bake in the oven for 20 minutes. Leave to cool and sprinkle with a little icing sugar. Arrange on a dish and serve.

Strawberry sauce for lemon ice cream (above); plum crescents (right)

Strawberry Sauce for Lemon Ice Cream
Gelato Rosato

To serve 4

1 lb/500 g lemon ice cream

8 oz/250 g fresh strawberries

3 tablespoons Cointreau liqueur

1 oz/25 g sugar

8 wafers

Preparation time: about 15 minutes plus 2 hours' soaking.

Keep the ice cream in the freezer for at least 2 hours before preparation. Rinse the strawberries in iced water, drain well and discard the hulls. Cut the strawberries into pieces and place them in a bowl. Pour on the Cointreau and sprinkle with the sugar. Cover the bowl and leave to soak for a couple of hours.

Just before you are ready to serve, purée the strawberries with their syrup to form a smooth sauce. Remove the ice cream from the freezer and, using a scoop, place balls of the ice cream either in a large serving goblet or in individual glasses. Coat the ice cream with the strawberry sauce and serve with the wafers.

Pudding with Almonds and Raisins

Crema Sformata con Mandorle e Uvetta

To serve 6

3 oz/75 g sultanas

¼ pint/150 ml dry white wine

4 oz/100 g almonds

2 eggs

6 oz/150 g caster sugar

2 slices white bread, crumbled

½ pint/250 ml light cream

½ pint/250 ml milk

ground nutmeg

1 teaspoon ground cinnamon

butter

Preparation and cooking time: about 1½ hours

Pre-heat the oven to 350°F/180°C/gas mark 4. Soak the sultanas in the white wine. Parboil the almonds in a little water for a few minutes, drain and peel them. Toast them in the oven for 3-4 minutes. Chop finely in a liquidiser.

Reduce the oven temperature to 300°F/150°C/gas mark 2. Beat the eggs, add the sugar and whisk to form soft peaks. Mix in the chopped almonds, the crumbled bread and the drained sultanas. Add the cream and milk and flavour with a pinch of ground nutmeg and a teaspoon of ground cinnamon. Butter a 10 inch/25 cm ovenproof pie dish and pour in the mixture. Cook in the pre-heated oven for at least 1 hour. The cake is ready when the centre is firm and springy to the touch. Cool in the dish and then turn on to a plate. This dish may be served with whipped cream piped on to the top or served separately.

Fried Ricotta Slices

Crema di Ricotta, Fritta

To serve 4-6

4 oz/100 g fresh Ricotta cheese

3 oz/75 g sugar

4 oz/100 g flour

5 eggs

⅓ pint/200 ml single cream

½ pint/300 ml milk

oil

a little semolina

Preparation and cooking time: about 40 minutes

Sieve and mash the Ricotta and mix it with the sugar, a little salt and the sifted flour. Stir in the eggs one at a time to form a smooth paste. Whisk in the cream and milk.

Heat the mixture in a small saucepan, stirring constantly with a whisk, and allow it to thicken. Remove from the heat as soon as it starts to boil.

Grease a baking pan with plenty of oil and pour in the mixture, spreading it to a thickness of about ½ inch. Leave to cool and set and then cut it into diamond shape. Coat the diamonds in the semolina.

Heat plenty of oil in a large frying pan and fry the diamonds a few at a time, turning them carefully so that they brown on all sides. Drain on kitchen paper and arrange on a plate. Serve warm or cold.

Fried ricotta slices

Profiteroles in Spun Caramel

Piramide di Bigné

To make about 40 profiteroles

For the pastries:

4 oz/100 g butter, cut into pieces

6 oz/150 g plain flour

4 eggs

a little butter

For the custard:

2 eggs plus 2 egg yolks

6 oz/150 g caster sugar

2 oz/50 g flour

1 pint/500 ml milk

1 sachet vanilla sugar

For the caramel:

6 oz/150 g caster sugar

Preparation and cooking time: about 2 hours

Bring to the boil a small saucepan containing ¼ pint/150 ml of water, the butter and a pinch of salt. As soon as it comes to the boil, remove it from the heat and pour in the sifted flour. Mix and return to the heat. Cook until the mixture no longer sticks to the edges of the pan and makes a slight crackling sound. Turn on to a working surface, spread out and leave to cool.

Pre-heat the oven to 375°F/190°C/gas mark 5. Return the mixture to the pan and mix in the eggs one at a time. When the mixture is smooth, spoon it into a piping bag. Pipe rosettes of the mixture on to a buttered baking tray, making sure that they are well separated – you should have enough mixture to make about 40 profiteroles. Bake in the oven for about 15 minutes. Before removing from the oven cut open 1 profiterole to check that it is cooked – it should be hollow and slightly crisp and golden in the centre. Cool the profiteroles on a wire rack.

Meanwhile, prepare the custard filling: beat 2 eggs, 2 extra yolks and the sugar until the mixture forms soft white peaks. Sift in the flour and add the cold milk and the vanilla sugar. Heat gently and allow to thicken, stirring constantly. As soon as the mixture comes to the boil, plunge the pan in cold water to cool. Pipe the mixture into the profiteroles and arrange them in a pyramid on a plate.

Prepare the caramel: melt the sugar in 4 tablespoons of water over a moderate heat. Let it boil until it has turned light brown, remove from the heat and stir to cool and thicken. When the caramel begins to form threads, pour it over the profiteroles, holding the pan fairly high and moving it in circles so that the caramel falls in spun threads around the profiteroles. If the caramel thickens too much, melt it gently over a low heat. Do not keep the profiteroles too long before serving or the caramel will soften.

Chocolate Gateau

Torta 'Gianfranco'

To serve 10

a little butter and flour

3 eggs plus 2 egg yolks

8 oz/250 g caster sugar

1 sachet vanilla sugar

10 oz/300 g plain cooking chocolate

4 oz/100 g flour

2 oz/50 g potato flour

3 tablespoons cocoa powder

baking powder

¼ pint/150 ml milk

¾ pint/400 ml whipping cream

2 oz/50 g flaked almonds

Preparation and cooking time: about 1¾ hours

Butter a 10 inch/25 cm round cake tin and sprinkle with flour. Whisk 3 eggs with 6 oz/150 g of the sugar, a pinch of salt and the vanilla sugar until they form soft peaks.

Pre-heat the oven to 350°F/180°C/gas mark 4. Melt 3 oz/75 g of the cooking chocolate on a low heat and leave to cool. Mix 4 oz/100 g of flour with the potato flour, cocoa and a heaped teaspoon of baking powder and sift into the egg mixture, folding it in carefully with a wooden spoon. Fold in the melted chocolate and pour the mixture into the prepared pan. Bake in the oven for about 30 minutes.

Meanwhile beat 2 egg yolks with the remaining flour, sugar and a pinch of salt. Gradually add the milk and bring to the boil, stirring constantly. Remove the pan from the heat and leave to cool, stirring from time to time.

Cut 4 oz/100 g of cooking chocolate into small pieces, melt it on a low heat and add it to the mixture, stirring vigorously. Leave to cool.

Turn the cake out on to a wire cooling rack. Whisk the cream until stiff and fold it into the chocolate mixture. Cut the cake into 3 equal layers and sandwich them together with two-thirds of the chocolate mixture. Coat the top and sides of the cake with chocolate mixture and sprinkle with the remainder of the cooking chocolate, grated.

Pipe rosettes of chocolate mixture on to the top of the cake and decorate with flaked almonds. Keep in the refrigerator and serve within 4-5 hours.

Profiteroles in spun caramel (top) and **chocolate gateau**

Panettone Charlotte
Charlotte di Panettone

To serve 8

about 1 lb/500 g apples

about 1½ lb/750 g pears

4 oz/100 g butter

4 oz/100 g sugar

¼ pint/150 ml dry white wine

12 oz/350 g panettone which has become a little hard

2 eggs

¼ pint/150 ml milk

6 tablespoons/100 ml cream

Preparation and cooking time: about 2½ hours plus cooling and chilling.

Pre-heat the oven to 350°F/180°C/gas mark 4. Peel, core and quarter the apples and pears. Heat 2 frying pans with about 2 oz/50 g of butter in each. As soon as the butter is hot, put the apples in one frying pan and the pears in the other. Sprinkle each with 1 tablespoon of sugar and pour half the wine into each frying pan. Cook over a low heat until the fruit is cooked but still firm and the pieces intact.

Meanwhile liberally butter a 3 pint/1.5 litre pudding basin, then cut 2 foil strips, about 2 inches/5 cm wide and long enough to place crosswise inside the basin with about ¾ inch/2 cm at the ends to hang over the rim. Butter these too. Cut the panettone into thin slices. Place a layer of panettone on the bottom of the basin and press it down lightly to make it stick. Then

place half the apples on top. Cover with another layer of panettone and then a layer of pears. Continue alternating the panettone, apples and pears in this way, finishing with a layer of panettone. Press down lightly so there are no spaces left.

Beat the eggs with the remaining sugar in a bowl and dilute with the milk and cream. Pour the mixture over the panettone and prick with a skewer to help the liquid penetrate. Leave the charlotte to rest for about 15 minutes, then bake for about 1½ hours. Remove from the oven and leave to cool. Then turn it out on to a serving dish with the help of the strips of foil (which should then be discarded). Refrigerate the charlotte for a couple of hours before serving. This is a good recipe for using up leftover panettone.

Chocolate and Amaretto Cup

Crema all'Amaretto

To serve 6-8

8 oz/250 g plain cooking chocolate

4 oz/100 g macaroons

4 egg yolks

4 oz/100 g sugar

3 oz/75 g flour

1½ pints/1 litre milk

1 sachet vanilla sugar

2 oz/50 g butter, cut into small pieces

2-3 tablespoons Amaretto liqueur

2 oz/50 g flaked almonds

Preparation and cooking time: about 50 minutes

Grate the chocolate and finely crush the macaroons. Whisk the egg yolks with the sugar until they form soft, whitish peaks. Fold in the sifted flour and 2 tablespoons of cold milk and stir until the mixture is smooth and free of lumps. Add the remaining milk and the vanilla sugar. Gently heat the mixture in a saucepan and bring it just to the boil, stirring constantly with a whisk. Cook for a few minutes, remove from the heat and stir in the butter, grated chocolate and crushed macaroons.

Pour the Amaretto liqueur into a serving bowl, making sure that the sides of the bowl are coated in the liqueur.

Pour in the prepared mixture and leave to cool. Top with the flaked almonds, cover with cling film and keep in the refrigerator until ready to serve.

Apple Fritters

Fritelle di Mele

To serve 6

butter

¼ oz/7 g fresh yeast

2 tablespoons milk

6 oz/150 g flour

1 oz/25 g cornflour

1 egg

1 tablespoon Calvados

1 oz/25 g caster sugar

about 6 tablespoons/100 ml light beer

1 lb/500 g apples, just ripe and not too large

oil for frying

icing or caster sugar

Preparation and cooking time: about 1 hour plus 2 hours' resting

Melt 1 oz/25 g of butter in a *bain-marie* and dissolve the yeast in the warm milk. Sift the flour and the cornflour together into a bowl. Make a well in the centre and put in a pinch of salt and the egg yolk, setting aside the white. Pour in the warm melted butter, the Calvados, sugar, yeast and milk. Using a wooden spoon, combine the ingredients in the centre of the well and when they are mixed together, start to incorporate the flour. Add the beer as the mixture becomes thicker. Finally, mix in 2 tablespoons of lukewarm water. Take care not to whisk vigorously, but stir continuously without lifting. Cover the dish and keep it in a slightly warm place for about 2 hours.

Whisk the reserved egg whites with a pinch of salt and carefully fold them into the batter, with an up-and-down rather than a circular movement. Heat a deep, heavy pan with plenty of oil. Peel and core the apples and cut them into rings about ¼ inch/5 mm thick. Dry them thoroughly between layers of kitchen paper then dip them, one at a time, in the batter. When the oil is hot but not boiling, immerse the battered apple rings and fry until they are golden brown on both sides. Drain them on a plate covered with a double layer of kitchen paper. Serve very hot, sprinkled with icing or caster sugar.

Chocolate and Amaretto cup

Festive Dove
Colomba Augurale

To serve 8

a little butter and flour

3 eggs

12 oz/350 g caster sugar

honey

1 sachet vanilla sugar

4 oz/100 g plain flour

2 oz/50 g potato flour

1 pint/500 ml milk

1 tea bag

6 egg yolks

Preparation and cooking time: about 1½ hours

Pre-heat the oven to 350°F/180°C/gas mark 4. Butter and flour a dove-shaped cake tin about 3 pints/1.5 litres in capacity. Whisk the 3 whole eggs with 6 oz/150 g of the sugar, ¼ teaspoon of honey, the vanilla sugar and a pinch of salt, until smooth and frothy. Mix the flour and potato flour and sift them into the sugar and egg mixture. Fold in with a wooden spoon using an up-and-down movement rather than a circular one so as not to deflate the mixture. Pour evenly into the tin and bake for about 30 minutes, until a skewer comes out clean. Remove the tin from the oven and, after a few minutes, turn the dove out on to a cooling rack.

While the cake is cooling, make the custard. Set aside 4 tablespoons of the milk and pour the rest into a saucepan. Bring gradually to the boil and remove from the heat. Put in the tea bag and leave to infuse for 5 minutes. Remove the tea bag, squeezing it thoroughly, and discard. Beat the egg yolks with the rest of the sugar until you obtain a frothy mixture. Then stir in first the reserved cold milk and then the tea-flavoured milk, poured in gradually through a fine strainer. Mix in with a small whisk. Heat the saucepan gently and bring the custard to just below boiling point, taking care not to let it actually boil. Remove from the heat at once and immerse in cold water, stirring continuously until the custard has cooled.

Pour the custard into a jug or bowl and serve with the dove. Decorate the dove as you please.

Fruit Fantasy
Fantasia di Frutta

To serve 2

3 firm, ripe mandarin oranges or clementines

2 kiwi fruits

1 small banana

2 red and 2 green maraschino cherries

1 tablespoon sugar

juice of ½ lemon

2 tablespoons liqueur of your choice

Preparation time: about 30 minutes

Wash and dry the mandarins, then cut them in half crosswise, use a grapefruit knife to loosen the flesh from the skin, without actually removing it. Peel the 2 kiwi fruits and slice them thinly into 16-18 slices. Cut the same number of slices from the banana and finally cut both the red and green cherries in half.

Arrange the 6 half-mandarins in the centre of 2 small oval-shaped dishes and decorate with the cherries. Put the slices of kiwi fruit round the outside, topped with the banana slices, and leave to rest for a few minutes (not in the refrigerator).

Meanwhile put the sugar in a bowl, add the strained lemon juice and stir until the sugar is dissolved. Mix this cold syrup with the liqueur, stir again, pour over the fruit and serve immediately.

Fruit fantasy

Orange Profiteroles

Bignoline al Fior d'Arancio

To serve 8-10

8 oz/250 g plain flour

½ teaspoon baking powder

2 oz/50 g granulated sugar

olive oil

1 tablespoon rum

grated rind of ½ lemon

2 eggs and 1 egg yolk

cooking oil

1 tablespoon orange flower water

3 tablespoons liquid honey

1 oz/25 g glucose powder

2 oz/50 g candied orange rind

10 peeled almonds

Preparation and cooking time: about 2 hours

Sift the flour and baking powder together. Make a well in the centre and place in it the sugar, the olive oil, the rum, the grated lemon rind, a pinch of salt, the eggs and egg yolk. Fold the ingredients into the flour and combine to a firm, smooth paste. Divide into small balls about the size of a hazelnut, place on a lightly oiled sheet of foil and leave to stand for 30 minutes.

Heat plenty of oil in a large deep-frying pan and fry the balls a few at a time. When they are golden brown, drain them on kitchen paper.

Put the orange flower water, the honey and the glucose powder into a large pan. Heat gently and stir until the ingredients have melted. Leave to cool and then add the candied orange rind, the chopped almonds and the prepared profiteroles. Stir well and heap on to a dish. Serve.

Crêpes with Custard Filling

Crespelle alla Crema d'Uovo

Makes 14 crêpes

4 very fresh eggs

4 oz/100 g plain flour

1 pint/500 ml milk

olive oil

4 oz/100 g caster sugar

1 sachet vanilla sugar

4 tablespoons/60 ml Cointreau liqueur

4 oz/100 g apricot or peach jam

Preparation and cooking time: about 45 minutes

Beat 2 of the eggs in a bowl together with the sieved flour and a pinch of salt. Gradually add half the cold milk, mixing continuously to prevent lumps forming. Heat a frying pan brushed lightly with olive oil. When it is hot, pour in a ladleful of the mixture and shake from side to side to ensure the entire surface of the pan is covered. Brown the crêpe on one side and then toss and continue heating for a few seconds. Turn the crêpe out on to a plate or marble surface and prepare a further 13 in the same way.

When the crêpes are ready, prepare the custard filling: in a small saucepan, beat the remaining 2 eggs with the sugar and sift in the remaining flour. Add the vanilla sugar, then the rest of the cold milk, gradually, stirring constantly. When smooth, place the saucepan over the heat and bring to the boil, stirring continuously. Remove from the heat and stir in the Cointreau and then cool by plunging the saucepan into cold water. Do not stop stirring. Spread the mixture on the crêpes and fold each one in four, then arrange on a serving dish. Heat the apricot jam with 1 tablespoon of water and simmer for a few seconds. Then brush the surface of the crêpes with this and serve.

Crêpes with custard filling

Venetian Cake with Cream and Chestnuts

Veneziana con Panna e Castagne

To serve 10

2¼ lb/1 kg large round brioche, panettone or plain cake

12 oz/350 g peeled, boiled chestnuts

4 oz/100 g plain chocolate

2 oz/50 g walnuts

½ pint/300 ml whipping cream

4 oz/100 g icing sugar

¼ pint/150 ml rum

1 marron glacé

Preparation time: about 1 hour
Cut the cake into 3 equal layers. Purée the peeled, boiled chestnuts. Finely chop the chocolate and the walnuts. Whip the cream until stiff, sift in 3 oz/ 75 g of the icing sugar, stirring with a top-to-bottom folding movement to avoid deflating the cream.

Place a layer of the cake on a serving plate, moisten it with half the rum, then spread it with half the whipped cream and half the chestnut purée, topped with half the chocolate and walnuts. Cover with the second layer of cake and fill in the same way. Cover with the top layer, place a small bowl in the centre and sprinkle the remaining icing sugar over the exposed surface of the cake. Remove the bowl and place the candied chestnut in the centre of the cake. Serve as soon as possible without refrigerating. The undecorated cake may be cut at first into several more layers in which case the filling ingredients are divided equally between all the layers.

Venetian cake with cream and chestnuts (top) and chestnut pagoda

Chestnut Pagoda
Pagoda di Castagne

To serve 8

8 oz/250 g chestnut purée

7 oz/200 g fresh Mascarpone cheese or cream cheese

4 oz/100 g icing sugar

1 oz/25 g cocoa powder

2 tablespoons brandy

3 tablespoons Amaretto

¼ pint/150 ml whipping cream

1 sponge cake, about 9 inches/23 cm in diameter, weighing 7 oz/200 g

6 tablespoons/100 ml Cointreau

1 tablespoon chocolate threads

1 tablespoon white chocolate chips

6 chocolate buttons

Preparation time: about 1½ hours
Place the chestnut purée in a bowl and mix in the Mascarpone cheese, stirring with a wooden spoon until smooth. Sift over it 3 oz/80 g of icing sugar and the cocoa powder, mix well, then add the brandy and Amaretto liqueur, making sure that each tablespoon is thoroughly absorbed before adding the next.

Whip the cream until firm, then fold in the rest of the sifted icing sugar stirring with a wooden spoon from top to bottom rather than round and round. Spoon into a piping bag with a small round nozzle, and keep in the refrigerator.

Place the sponge cake on a serving dish and moisten it with the Cointreau, then sieve on to it the mixture of chestnuts and Mascarpone cheese, arranging it in a small heap. Pipe the sweetened whipped cream around the edge, and sprinkle over the chocolate threads. Complete the decoration of the cake by placing the white chocolate chips on top of it and the chocolate buttons evenly spread around it.

Keep the cake in the least cold part of the refrigerator until serving time. If you wish, instead of using sponge cake as a base, you can use any other risen cake such as panettone, viennese pastry and so on.

Macaroon Grape Tart
Sfogliata Amarettata all'Uva

To serve 10

10 oz/300 g puff pastry

butter

6 small macaroons

4 tablespoons/60 ml red vermouth

about 18 oz/500 g white grapes

1 egg

3 oz/75 g caster sugar

¾ oz/20 g flour

1 envelope vanilla sugar

⅓ pint/200 ml milk

Preparation and cooking time: about 1¼ hours plus any thawing
Defrost the pastry if necessary. Roll it out and use it to line a buttered round 10 inch/26 cm pie dish. Prick the bottom with a fork, then sprinkle over 5 finely crumbled macaroons. Moisten with the red vermouth and leave in a cool place. Pre-heat the oven to 375°F/190°C/gas mark 5.

Wipe the grapes with a damp cloth. Break the egg into a small saucepan, add 2 oz/50 g of sugar, the sieved flour and the vanilla sugar. Whisk to prevent lumps forming, then dilute the mixture with the cold milk, poured in a thin stream.

Bring the mixture to the boil, stirring all the time, then immediately pour it over the macaroons. Arrange the grapes on top, pushing them down slightly, in 4 concentric circles. Crumble the remaining macaroons and sprinkle over the centre of the pie. Place a single grape in the middle.

Put the remaining sugar into a small saucepan with a tablespoon of cold water, simmer for a few moments until you have a fairly thick syrup, then brush the grapes with it. Place the pie in the pre-heated oven for about 40 minutes, then remove and allow to cool in the mould before turning out and serving.

Oranges in Grand Marnier

Oranges in Grand Marnier
Arance al Grand Marnier

To serve 4

6 large ripe oranges, washed

6 sugar cubes

4 tablespoons Grand Marnier

Preparation and cooking time: about 30 minutes plus 30 minutes' refrigeration
Pierce the oranges all over with a needle. Rub every side of a sugar cube over each orange. Place the sugar in a saucepan. Peel the oranges, remove all the pith and divide them into segments in a bowl. Squeeze any juice remaining in the peel over the sugar cubes.

Heat the sugar gently until dissolved. When a light syrup has formed, remove the pan from the heat and pour in the Grand Marnier. Stir and allow to cool. Pour the liquid over the orange segments and refrigerate for 30 minutes before serving. If you like, you can place the oranges in individual goblets and garnish each one with a green grape.

September Fruit Salad

Capriccio Settembrino

To serve 4

2 apples

juice of 1 lemon

2 oz/50 g sugar

1 peach

¾ lb/350 g Victoria plums

½ lb/250 g green grapes

3 tablespoons Cointreau

Preparation time: about 30 minutes plus 1 hour's refrigeration

Peel and core the 2 apples, cut into quarters and then dice. As they are ready, put them into a bowl containing the strained lemon juice. Add the sugar, then mix carefully with a wooden spoon.

Remove the stalks from the peach and the plums and wipe with a damp cloth. Cut in half and remove the stones, then dice and add to the apples in the bowl. Wipe the grapes with a damp cloth and remove stalks and pips. Cut the larger grapes in half. Add to the rest of the fruit. Mix well and pour over the Cointreau. Cover with cling film and refrigerate for at least 1 hour. Mix carefully before serving.

Redcurrant and Lemon Cream Baskets

'Cestini' Con Crema e Ribes

To serve 4

5 large unblemished lemons

2 small macaroons

3 egg yolks

4 oz/100 g sugar

1 oz/25 g flour

½ pint/300 ml milk

1 tablespoon lemon liqueur

8 bunches redcurrants

8 fresh mint leaves

7 rolled wafers

Preparation and cooking time: about 1 hour

Wash and grate the rind of one lemon into a saucepan. Halve the other 4 lemons and squeeze them, reserving the juice for other uses. With a sharp knife, scrape out the flesh, leaving them smooth. Flatten the bases so that they will stand level.

Crumble the macaroons and divide them among the half-lemons. Add to the pan with the lemon rind the 3 egg yolks, the sugar, the flour and 2 tablespoons of the milk, and beat to obtain a perfectly smooth mixture. Add the rest of the cold milk and, stirring all the time, bring the custard to boiling point. Remove from the heat and flavour with a tablespoon of lemon liqueur, then stand the pan in cold water and continue to stir until the custard is completely cooled.

Wash the redcurrants in ice-cold water and dry them on a cloth. Pick off the largest currants and arrange them over the macaroon crumbs in the lemon halves; fill up with the lemon cream, using a piping bag with a plain round nozzle. Garnish each lemon half with a bunch of redcurrants and a mint leaf and arrange on a flat dish, interspersed with the wafers. Serve immediately, before the cream can absorb any bitterness from the lemon pith.

If you do not wish to use lemon halves as containers for this recipe, you could substitute individual puff pastry or shortcrust pie shells baked blind with dried beans to keep them in shape. The baskets will still need to be served quickly, before the pastry loses its crispness.

Stuffed Baked Apples
Mele Golose

To serve 10

1 oz/25 g almonds, blanched

1 oz/25 g hazelnuts, blanched

1 oz/25 g groundnuts, blanched

1 oz/25 g walnuts, blanched

1 oz/25 g plain chocolate, broken into pieces

10 apples, equal in size and not too ripe

butter

1 small cinnamon stick

3 cloves

spiral of lemon rind, 3 inches/7.5 cm long

¼ pint/150 ml Muscat wine

6 oz/150 g caster sugar

4 egg yolks

1 oz/25 g cornflour

a little vanilla sugar

1 pint/500 ml milk

4 tablespoons Calvados

1 oz/25 g pistachio nuts

¼ pint/125 ml whipping cream

Preparation and cooking time: about 1½ hours plus refrigeration

Pre-heat the oven to 375°F/190°C/gas mark 5. Put the almonds, hazelnuts, groundnuts, walnuts and chocolate into a liquidiser and process at maximum speed for a few seconds until the ingredients are all ground to a paste. Put the mixture in a bowl. Peel the apples, and, using an apple corer, cut into the base, stopping when you reach the stalk: you should hollow out the core just up to the stalk end, leaving it closed at the top. Remove the apple flesh from the cores, chop it and add to the ground nuts in the bowl, and mix well.

Stuff each apple with the mixture, pressing it in with a teaspoon. Butter an ovenproof dish which is just the right size to hold the apples and arrange them in it. Break up the cinnamon stick and put this in the dish, along with the cloves and the lemon rind. Pour in the Muscat wine and sprinkle over 2 oz/50 g of sugar. Bake in the oven for about 45 minutes, basting from time to time with the juices.

Remove the cooked apples from the oven and set them aside while you prepare the custard. Beat the egg yolks in a saucepan with the remaining sugar and a pinch of salt. Then pour in the milk in a slow trickle, mixing constantly with a small whisk. Bring to the boil, remove from the heat and add the Calvados. Arrange the apples on a serving dish and pour over the custard at once.

Blanch the pistachio nuts in boiling salted water, chop them and sprinkle them over the custard-covered apples. Whip the cream until it is stiff and put in a piping bag. Decorate the apples with swirls around the outside and one in the centre. Keep in a very cool place or in the least cold part of the refrigerator until you are ready to serve.

Grape and Apple Cheesecake
Crostata di Mascarpone all'Uva e Mela

To serve 8

For the crust:

4 oz/100 g flour

2 oz/50 g caster sugar

4 oz/100 g butter

2 egg yolks

grated rind of 1 lemon

a little butter and flour

For the filling:

7 oz/200 g Mascarpone cheese

2 oz/50 g icing sugar

2 egg yolks

2 tablespoons brandy

For the topping:

20 small macaroons

a large bunch green grapes

1 apple

5 tablespoons caster sugar

5 mint leaves

Preparation and cooking time: about 1½ hours

To make the crust: put the sifted flour, sugar and a pinch of salt together in a bowl and add the butter, cut in small cubes. Rub it in with your fingers until the mixture resembles coarse breadcrumbs. Add the egg yolks and the lemon rind. Roll the pastry into a ball, wrap it in cling film and leave it in the least cold part of the refrigerator for 30 minutes.

Meanwhile pre-heat the oven to 375°F/190°C/gas mark 5. Grease and flour a round 10 inch/25 cm pie dish with a smooth bottom and fluted sides. Roll out the pastry and line the pan, pricking the bottom with a fork. Bake in the oven for about 20 minutes or until well cooked and golden. Leave to cool in the tin.

Meanwhile, prepare the filling: beat the cheese and sugar together, incorporating the egg yolks one at a time. Add the brandy.

Crumble the macaroons finely. When the pie shell is cold, take it out of the pan and set it on a plate. Sprinkle the macaroons over the bottom and pour in the filling. Wash and dry the grapes and arrange them on top together with thin slices of apple.

Dissolve 5 tablespoons of sugar in 1 tablespoon of water over a low heat. When it is a thick syrup, brush it, still hot, over the fruit. Decorate the centre of the cake with the mint leaves and keep it in a cool place or the least cold part of the refrigerator. Serve within a couple of hours.

Grape and apple cheesecake

Coffee Ice Cream
Gelato al Caffè

To serve 6

2 oz/50 g coffee

1 envelope vanilla sugar

12 oz/350 g granulated sugar

⅓ pint/200 ml single cream

1 egg white

Preparation and cooking time: 30 minutes plus freezing time
In a small saucepan bring 12 fl oz/350 ml of water to the boil, pour in the coffee and, stirring constantly, simmer over a very low heat until the foam has disappeared. Leave to infuse for about 15 minutes, so that the ground coffee sinks to the bottom of the saucepan, then strain the liquid coffee into a bowl.

Add the vanilla sugar and the sugar, stir until the sugar is dissolved then leave to cool. At this point mix in the cream and place in the refrigerator for at least 1 hour to cool completely.

Pour the mixture into an ice-cream machine or container, add the egg white whisked to a froth, with a pinch of salt, so that the ice-cream will be smooth and soft.

Ricotta Pie with Sultanas
Torta di Ricotta alla Panna

To serve 8

12 oz/350 g shortcrust pastry

a little flour

a little butter

2 oz/50 g sultanas

4 oz/100 g candied peel

12 oz/350 g full-cream Ricotta

3 eggs

4 oz/100 g sugar

grated rind of 1 lemon

a little icing sugar

Preparation and cooking time: about 1 hour plus thawing
Defrost the pastry if necessary. Roll out the pastry on a lightly floured board and use it to line a buttered, floured 11 inch/28 cm pie dish. Cut off the excess dough and shape into a ring with which to thicken the sides of the pie; then prick the base with a fork.

Pre-heat the oven to 350°F/180°C/gas mark 4. Wash and dry the sultanas; cut the candied peel into small cubes. Sieve the Ricotta into a bowl and mix in, one at a time, the yolks of the three eggs, then the sugar, the grated rind of the lemon, the diced candied peel and the sultanas, stirring vigorously. Beat the egg whites with a pinch of salt until they are quite firm and fold them into the mixture.

Pour the mixture into the pastry shell and tap the dish to remove air bubbles in the mixture. Bake for about 45 minutes. Finally, turn out and leave it to cool. Before serving sprinkle with icing sugar.

Ricotta pie with sultanas

Meringue Gateau

Torta Meringata

To serve 10

For the meringue:

a little almond oil

3 egg whites

8 oz/250 g icing sugar

a little vanilla sugar

For the éclairs:

butter

2 oz/50 g flour

1 egg

For the custard:

3 eggs

4 oz/100 g sugar

a little vanilla sugar

2 oz/50 g plain flour

1 pint/500 ml milk

1 tablespoon cocoa powder

1 tablespoon Grand Marnier

1 tablespoon Maraschino

6 tablespoons/100 ml whipping cream

Preparation and cooking time: about 4 hours

To prepare the meringue: lightly grease an 11 inch/28 cm circle of greaseproof paper with a little almond oil and place it on a small baking tray. Pre-heat the oven to 225°F/190°C/gas mark 5. Whisk the egg whites with a pinch of salt and sieve in 7 oz/200 g of icing sugar and the vanilla sugar, a little at a time, beating briskly until the mixture is well risen and firm. Using a piping bag with a round nozzle, cover the circle of greaseproof paper by piping two overlapping spirals. Sprinkle the remaining icing sugar on top and bake for a couple of hours; then turn off the oven and leave an hour before taking it out to cool.

To prepare the éclairs: pre-heat the oven to 375°F/190°C/gas mark 5, butter and flour a small baking tray. Bring 4 tablespoons of water to the boil in a saucepan with 1 oz/25 g of diced butter and a pinch of salt. As soon as

the butter is completely melted, remove from the heat and sieve in the flour, beating briskly with a wooden spoon. Return the pan to the heat and continue to cook, stirring continuously, until the mixture begins to sizzle. Turn it on to a plate and spread it out to cool.

Return it to the pan and beat in the egg, making sure the mixture is completely smooth. Using a piping bag with a round nozzle, make at least 30 walnut-sized blobs on the prepared baking tray. Bake for 15 minutes then turn out to cool on a wire rack.

To prepare the custard: beat the 3 eggs, the sugar, the vanilla sugar, the flour and a pinch of salt together in a saucepan. When smooth, gradually add the milk. Bring to the boil, stirring all the time. Remove from the heat and divide into two, adding the cocoa powder and Grand Marnier to one half and the Maraschino to the other. Let them cool, stirring frequently, then put them into 2 separate piping bags with round nozzles.

To assemble the gateau: whip the cream and pipe it into the eclairs, then sprinkle them with a little icing sugar. Just before serving, set the meringue base on a large plate, make a ring round the edge with the yellow custard and set the eclairs on it. Cover the rest of the meringue with alternate stripes of the two custards and serve.

Sunshine Fruit Salad

Macedonia Solare

To serve 6

1 large slice ripe watermelon, weighing about 1¼ lb/600 g

2 tablespoons white rum

a small bunch of black grapes

1 oz/25 g sugar

1 tablespoon Cointreau

3 large yellow peaches (not too ripe)

juice of ½ lemon

fresh mint leaves for garnish

Preparation time: about 1¼ hours

Using a potato scoop or melon-baller, make small, equal-sized balls from the slice of watermelon. Discard any seeds, place the melon balls in a bowl and sprinkle with the white rum; cover the bowl with cling film and refrigerate for about 30 minutes.

Wash and dry the grapes, and remove the best ones. Place them in a small bowl, sprinkle with a tablespoon of sugar and with 2 tablespoons of Cointreau, then set them aside to rest in a cool place or in the least cold part of the refrigerator, for about 15 minutes.

Wash and dry the peaches, cut them into thin slices and drop them into a bowl; sprinkle with a tablespoon of sugar and the strained juice of half a lemon. Mix gently, cover the bowl and place it in the least cold part of the refrigerator for about 15 minutes.

A short while before serving, arrange the fruit in circles on a large serving dish, garnish with leaves of fresh mint and the reserved grapes and serve.

INDEX